# F. Scott Fitzgerald

# F. Scott Fitzgerald

## Richard Shephard

www.pocketessentials.com

This edition published in 2005 by Pocket Essentials
P.O.Box 394, Harpenden, Herts, AL5 1XJ

www.pocketessentials.com

Distributed in the USA by Trafalgar Square Publishing,
P.O. Box 257, Howe Hill Road, North Pomfret, Vermont 05053

A CIP catalogue record for this book is available from the British Library.

ISBN 1 904048 40 4

2 4 6 8 10 9 7 5 3 1

Typeset by Avocet Typeset, Chilton, Aylesbury, Bucks
Printed and bound in Great Britain by Cox & Wyman, Reading

To Jo, with love and thanks. Gggrrr!

# Contents

# Introduction

**Show me a hero and
I will write you a tragedy.**

F. Scott Fitzgerald wrote this memorable line probably in
the early 1930s, jotting it down in his notebooks during a
period when his life was starting to unravel and his confidence in his writing beginning to crumble. For just over
two decades, however, he did exactly that, presenting a
continuous tragedy that ran, not just through his work, but
also throughout his short life. Of all his many achieve-
ments, perhaps his most remarkable was his unerring ability
to write prose that has survived the mythic extremes and
excesses of his legend and reputation and, in the years since
his death, has flourished to such an amazing degree that it
now stands as a pinnacle of twentieth century literature.
Although it is ultimately the writing that matters, so
complex is the relationship between his work and his life,
that it's virtually impossible to view them separately, a state
of affairs that has fascinated and obsessed both his admirers
and critics over the years. Despite his own assertion that
'There never was a good biography of a novelist. There
couldn't be. He is too many people, if he's any good',
Fitzgerald has been the subject of over eighty books, more

9

than of any other modern writer, and even critical works have included substantial biographical content. Foremost among these scholars and biographers is Matthew J Bruccoli, who in his introduction to *F Scott Fitzgerald: A Life in Letters*, summed up the link between Fitzgerald's life and writing simply and eloquently: 'Everything F Scott Fitzgerald wrote was a form of autobiography.'

Fitzgerald's abilities as a chronicler of the first forty years of the twentieth century remain unparalleled and perhaps it should come as no great surprise that his art and life are so inextricably linked, since, in writing about these years, he was reflecting what he saw, perceived and *felt* of American society. To this effect, he and his writing thrived and dazzled in the 1920s, faltered and lost direction in the 1930s, just like the rest of the country and much of Europe. It could be argued that part of the reason that Fitzgerald's portrayal of America, certainly in the 1920s, is so accurate is because he gives the impression of having invented it. At any rate, he named it, calling it the Jazz Age, and peopled it with a cast of flappers, bootleggers, impresarios, young lovers, gangsters, soldiers, artists, Broadway and Hollywood stars, killers and ordinary folk caught up in a life that had never seemed so fast. New York in the 1920s was the perfect place to find such a cast, and he skilfully assembled it from the kaleidoscope that he witnessed whirling around him: newspapers, magazines, his own friends, a vast array of celebrities, the movies, speakeasies and of course, his biggest inspiration – Zelda. Somehow, despite being caught up in, even at the vortex of, this fierce, relentless whirlpool, he was able to capture it on paper, and do so hundreds of times.

In spite of Ernest Hemingway's and his friend Sara Murphy's joint accusation that Fitzgerald didn't understand people or have, in her words, 'the faintest idea what anybody else but yourself is like', he had exceptionally sensitive social antennae and his ability to capture moods and nuances was faultless, and revealed in countless examples in his fiction. Alongside this, he also had the felicitous knack of sprinkling a bit of magic onto everything he did, so that even his most commonplace and commercial writing glimmers with a radiance that was his alone.

Because of his fame, notoriety and, at times, astonishing success, critics have found it difficult to take him seriously as a novelist, something that plagued him until his death, but, really, there is no American writer who is finer. Anyone, whether author or reader, who is still in pursuit of that hoary old beast, the Great American Novel, should read *The Great Gatsby*, and abandon the chase immediately. Fitzgerald's early success, however, along with his and Zelda's youth and glamour, and their taste for the recently Prohibited alcohol, almost obscured the brilliance of his writing. This critical blinkeredness may have been helped into place by his astonishing prolificity and the seeming ease with which he wrote, particularly his stories. Often derided, particularly by their author, for having jeopardized his standing as a novelist, Fitzgerald's stories actually represent a major part of his talent, and without doubt, until his third and final sojourn in Hollywood, they financed his life and career. Including his early work, written for school publications, he produced 164 stories, which were sold to a wide range of magazines, and there are only eight, written in the last five years of Fitzgerald's life, that have never been published in collections. These, according to his daughter, Scottie Fitzgerald Smith, are best left unread by present and future generations.

Fitzgerald's career was as paradoxical as his life, since, while aware that he could only hope to achieve literary greatness through his novels, he knew that the stories were his real means of earning money, and in ever increasing sums. His story price with *The Saturday Evening Post*, for instance, rose from $400 to a peak of $4,000 in just ten years, and in 1929, the year in which it jumped from $3,500 to $4,000, he earned, minus agent's commissions, $27,000 from new stories, while the income from all of his books for the year was a (potentially) sobering $31.17. Multiplying these sums by ten will give their approximate worth in today's money, and this illustrates just how successful (and, sadly, how wasteful) Fitzgerald was in his prime. Even so, he appeared to be writing these lucrative stories just to pay off his debts, instead of using them to shore up money and time to devote to his next novel.

One of the great tragedies of his life was that he seemed unable to realise that he had the chance of having both an extremely comfortable existence and an enduring immortality, or, rather, he seemed incapable of moderating his chaotic lifestyle so that he could achieve both of these aims. Critics who concur with Fitzgerald's dismissal of his stories also fail to realize that his depiction of America rests largely on the strength of these, since they were written in a short space of time, sometimes overnight, and provide an instant snapshot of the times, whereas the novels, even something as short and perfectly-formed as *The Great*

*Gatsby*, were usually written, and rewritten, over a period of two years or so.

In his introduction to *Babylon Revisited—The Screenplay*, the published script that Fitzgerald had adapted from his magnificent story of the same name, and which was actually re-titled *Cosmopolitan*, Budd Schulberg notes that 'Fitzgerald's life and career seemed to stagger from irony to irony'. While it's interesting to see that Schulberg also treats this 'life and career' as if it were a single entity, his point about the landmarks of irony that Fitzgerald repeatedly encountered in his brief journey, is right on the money. The most profound irony of all, of course, is that Fitzgerald died in the belief that he was a failure and that his writing would be forgotten. Neither he, nor Zelda, in fact, were alive to witness the astonishing success of his books, which continues to the present day, with over twenty million copies sold around the world in the last sixty years or so. This makes an average of about 333,000 books a year. Not too shabby for a failure, and a dead one, at that.

Writing in a 1938 letter to his editor and friend, Maxwell Perkins, after his first novel, *This Side of Paradise* had gone out of print, Fitzgerald admitted, with his customary mixture of pride and self-depreciation, that he was beginning 'to feel somewhat neglected. Isn't my reputation being allowed to let slip away? I mean what's left of it.' In 1940, seven months before he died, he wrote again to Perkins, unhappy that *The Great Gatsby* would die and he would disappear, wistfully wondering if his masterpiece had already '*had* its chance', and bemoaning the unfairness of the fact that he seemed destined to be forgotten as an author, despite his talent: 'Even now, there is little published in American fiction that doesn't slightly bear my stamp – in a small way I was an original.'

In one sense he was wrong, of course, since he was an original in countless ways and remains one of the most influential writers of twentieth century prose. In 1999, almost seventy-five years after the book was first published, in a list of the greatest novels published in the last hundred years, as selected by authors, scholars and critics for the Modern American Library, *The Great Gatsby* came second, just under James Joyce's *Ulysses*. In a similar list, instigated as a response to the male-oriented first one, and chosen mainly by women in their twenties at Radcliffe College, Fitzgerald's novel actually came *first*. How's that for immortality? In the Modern Library list, even his flawed masterpiece, *Tender is the Night*, was at twenty-eighth place. To put this into perspective, it's interesting to compare Fitzgerald's positions with those of his erstwhile friend and rival, Ernest Hemingway. Hemingway's *The Sun Also Rises* came in at forty-fifth place, while his *A Farewell to Arms* reached seventy-fourth place. Such a reckoning is a far cry from the days when Fitzgerald wrote of himself and Hemingway: 'I talk with the authority of failure – Ernest with the authority of success. We could never sit across the same table again.' Once again he was wrong, in that those positions of failure and success are now reversed.

At the time of writing, a stage adaptation of his second novel, *The Beautiful and Damned*, is attracting audiences in London's West End, while *The New York Times*, hoping to draw in readers and advertising dollars, is serializing his third novel, *The Great Gatsby*. Sponsored, perhaps appropriately, by a group of New York BMW dealers, this will be the first time Fitzgerald's most brilliant novel has been serialized, since it was turned down by *Liberty* magazine in 1925 on account of its quota of adultery and killing, deemed too racy for a publication aimed mainly at women. (An offer of a much needed $10,000 from *College Humor* was rejected by Fitzgerald, who wrote to his agent, Harold Ober, complaining that people 'would be sure that Gatsby was a great halfback and that would kill it in book form.' The other problem was that serializing the novel in any magazine would take several months and delay publication, which was the last thing Fitzgerald wanted.)

Further proof of just how tenaciously Fitzgerald's spell lingers can be found in the way his words have infiltrated popular consciousness, cropping up regularly in newspapers and magazines. A recent book review in the film periodical *Sight and Sound*, for example, opened with Fitzgerald's memorable quotation: 'There are no second acts in American lives', and this same line also headed an article about the death of Marlon Brando in *The Guardian*. (Curiously, the newspaper omitted any quotation marks, although whether this was because Fitzgerald's quote has become so famous that it's now treated as a piece of folk wisdom, or was simply a result of the newspaper's notorious typographic inconsistency is unknown.) All of this merely confirms what has been apparent for almost a century, that no one could say it quite like Fitzgerald. Even though, as he once said, 'the two basic stories of all times are *Cinderella* and *Jack the Giant Killer* – the charm of women and the courage of men', he found a way of spinning these two stories out infinitely and exquisitely, adorning them with every bright bauble and every shadow, every bit of truth his heart and imagination could muster.

# Part One:
# The Early Years: 1896 – 1919

# Childhood and School

Francis Scott Fitzgerald was born in St Paul, Minnesota, on 24 September 1896, the same year that movies and ragtime first appeared in New York, and a little over three years before the beginning of the twentieth century, arguably the century of America, and a period he would write about and, in some small way, create, with such resonance, wit and charm. Drawn to European literature and its sensitivities, he was nevertheless a consummate American writer, and was named after his ancestor, Francis Scott Key, the composer of *The Star Spangled Banner*, about as American a forebear as one could get. He was the only son of Edward Fitzgerald, a pleasant and kind, if rather unlucky, man, and Mary McQuillan Fitzgerald, an energetic, eccentric woman whose Irish family had a substantial sum of money and who looked down on the more genteel, but humble, Fitzgeralds. Edward Fitzgerald owned an unsuccessful wicker furniture business but he was a poor businessman and an ineffectual provider for his family. His meagre efforts to support them, often derided by his wife, had to be backed up by her money.

Fitzgerald was the third child of the marriage, born a few months after the deaths of his two elder sisters in an epidemic, and the elder brother to Annabel, born five years later. He was spoiled by his indulgent, but erratic mother, while his father, whose side he took, struggled to be a salesman. After his furniture business went under, Edward Fitzgerald worked for Procter and Gamble, but he was sacked suddenly, aged fifty-five, and returned home, as his son described in an interview after his father's death, 'an old man, a completely broken man', who was 'a failure the rest of his days'. His father was humiliatingly obliged to rely on McQuillan money, and to make things worse, when his eleven-year-old son heard this distressing news, he was horrified, and cried, 'Dear God, please don't let us go to the poorhouse; please don't let us go to the poorhouse'.

Following this, the Fitzgeralds were obliged to move around until they settled in a rather dreary house on Summit Avenue, where, in the attic, Fitzgerald would complete his first novel, *This Side of Paradise*, in 1919, an event that he would record in a brief bit of verse in a letter.

> 'In a house below the average
> Of a street above the average
> In a room above the roof.'

This background of class and historical lineage on his father's side, money and Irish eccentricity on his mother's was already fermenting in the young Fitzgerald, so that the rather chaotic and humbling travails of his home life, and his need to dissimulate and create a better, if not perfect, world for himself, were starting to simmer away in the crucible of his imagination. Of the many themes that resonate in his fiction, two dominate: love and money. He received the former from his father and the latter had its origin with his mother and her family. She spoiled and pampered him, trying to make him a success, no doubt to overcome the disappointment she felt in her husband, but she didn't bother to discipline him or teach him the modesty and self-restraint he might have found assets in later life. Clearly, his parents failed to live up to his, no doubt, exacting standards, being less glamorous, less prosperous, less effective and, in the case of his mother, less normal than he wanted them to be.

At a camp, when he was ten years old and separated from them for the first time, he was bullied and miserable, and wrote and told them. His father sent him a dollar and some paternal advice on how to spend it, while his mother threatened to visit him. Shrewdly, he dissuaded her from coming, but succeeded in getting another dollar out of her by making good use of his father's advice and promising her he would 'spend it cautiously'. Pointedly, he added that, 'All the other boys have pocket money besides their regular allowance'. Along with other letters written during his childhood, all asking his beleaguered parents for cash, because 'all my money is used up' (the impersonal tone is a nice touch, suggesting it's the money's fault and not his), this letter points straight to the adult Fitzgerald a few years down the line, when he was an author regularly imploring both his publisher and his agent to advance him money for stories and novels he hadn't yet written. A year or two prior to this, when he was struggling to be a copywriter at the Barron Collier advertising agency and failing to get his stories published, he felt understandably bitter, because he was broke and his fiancée, Zelda Sayre, had broken off their engagement. His prospects were poor, and she had reluctantly ceased, or postponed, trusting in his ability to make something of his life. Since he had no money to back him up, or, crucially, to support them should she ever decide to join him in New York, Zelda, a well-to-do Southern girl with one eye on a string of even more well-to-do potential suitors, had lost faith in him and his ability to support them both. This painful, even brutal, experience would be reworked again and again in his fiction, ironically generating thousands of dollars for Fitzgerald.

After his lowly experiences at camp, he began at St Paul Academy where, within a year, he had written his first stories and had begun to participate in the activities that were always to hold a fascination for him and for which he had an affinity. These included socially-inclined activities like dancing (classes that his mother made him take, since she knew he would meet children from the most prestigious – or rather, wealthy – families) and sports like basketball and football, at which he wanted desperately to shine, knowing instinctively how heroic this would be, but for which he was too slight. Sometimes the other children would arrive in large limousines and be driven by chauffeurs in liveried uniform, no doubt watched by a Fitzgerald just on the verge of adolescence, a boy who was already casting himself as the hero in the stories he was starting to write. (Around twenty years later, when he was in Europe, basking in the afterglow of critical acclaim for *The Great Gatsby* and its success as a Broadway play, and the royalties this generated, and during a period when he started receiving three and a half thousand dollars for each story published in *The Saturday Evening Post*, he would temporarily abandon the struggle he was having in writing his fourth novel and knock out a whole series of tales about Basil Duke Lee, a schoolboy alter ego, and his female counterpart, Josephine. These stories, about 120,000 words in all, covered the years from 1907, when their author was eleven, to 1913, when he was seventeen and about to enter Princeton University.)

He joined in amateur dramatics and quickly took over, as writer, director and, naturally, leading man. Every summer for four years, with increasing success, he would write and act in a play for the local company, the Elizabethan Dramatic Club. In 1911, he was sent to the Newman School, a Catholic institution in New Jersey, where he would be a boarder, and, so his parents hoped, would both learn some discipline and improve his grades. Less than an hour from New York, the school must have seemed a real step forward to Fitzgerald, who was becoming frustrated by the comparatively provincial St Paul. Within a short time, he was thoroughly disliked, ostracized and utterly miserable, a gloomy experience that he worked neatly into his first novel, *This Side of Paradise*, whose hero, Amory Blaine shares many of the hardships from which Fitzgerald suffered. 'He went all wrong at the start, was generally considered both conceited and arrogant, and was universally detested.' Amory, like his creator, was 'unbearably lonely, desperately unhappy ... confined to bounds, unpopular with both faculty and students'. Much of this misery is also evoked in *The Freshest Boy*, a story written for the *Basil* series in 1928, sixteen years later. Even as a youth, and at the height of his unhappiness, he was able to turn personal tragedy into an artistic triumph, by writing about the unkindnesses that life seemed to have in store for him. A poem, cannily entitled *Football*, about an incident when he was unfairly accused of cowardice in a game, was published in the school magazine, the *Newman News*. After this, things gradually improved for Fitzgerald, as he worked harder on his poor grades, made friends with a boy who was a school football hero, improved at sports, acted in a school play and had stories published in the magazine. In his second year, he met and was befriended by Father Sigourney Fay, a recently converted Catholic, who was a member of the school board and was soon to be appointed its director. He became the young Fitzgerald's mentor, father figure and spiritual guide and was transposed into the pages of *This Side of Paradise* as Monsignor Darcy. Fay's friendship and influence helped Fitzgerald to become a more rounded individual, the 'personage' that his protagonist Amory Blaine becomes in *This Side of Paradise*, and thus prepared him for his entrance to Princeton, the first real turning point in his young and somewhat haphazard life.

That he ever went to Princeton was down to the death of his grandmother, who had bequeathed a substantial estate, worth $125,000, which provided the financially ailing Fitzgeralds with significant fiscal security. Rather than going to the less expensive, but fairly drab, University of Minnesota, Fitzgerald could now attend whichever college he preferred. He gave several reasons for his choice, but the main one was that, while near the end of his time at Newman, he had found the score for a musical comedy on a piano. Entitled *His Honor the Sultan*, it had been presented by the Triangle Club of Princeton University, and the young student, with a modicum of dramatic success himself, and with passionate memories of those evenings when sufficient cramming had allowed him to leave his studies and venture out to New York to see a Broadway musical, was won over. As he put it, years later: 'That was enough for me. From then on, the university question was settled. I was bound for Princeton.'

Needless to say, it wasn't that simple. His love of football and the fact that he had watched a Princeton–Harvard game in 1911 (where Princeton's full-back made a valiant eighty-five yard dash to score the winning touchdown, sending Fitzgerald into a frenzy of excitement) must have played their part. Now that his family had sufficient sums to enable him to enter Princeton, the balance of Fitzgerald's academic account was less impressive. Though he failed the written exam, he made up for it in an oral test, and, won over by his eloquence and his Irish charm, the examiners decided to give him a chance. On his seventeenth birthday, he was accepted into Princeton.

# Princeton: 1913–1917

Just as Monsignor Fay had had a profound affect on Fitzgerald at Newman, so too, at Princeton, did Christian Gauss, the head of the modern languages department, and one of the very few professors there who was able to snare Fitzgerald's admiration, or even attention. Some of his other teachers were dismissive of his wavering application and what they considered his lack of interest, and one of them, later the head of the department, continually refused to believe that this indifferent student was the same man who had written *The Great Gatsby*.

Other than Gauss, his real mentors were two friends, John Peale Bishop, who was his classmate and Edmund Wilson, who was in the year above them. Always a voracious reader, Fitzgerald had, for the first time, encountered friends and peers with whom he could discuss books and writers. Amory Blaine, in *This Side of Paradise*, meets and airily discusses 'books he had read, read about, books he had never heard of', with a young man called Thomas Parke D'Invilliers, who is 'partly taken in and wholly delighted' with his new acquaintance. (The verse epigraph, before the dedication to Zelda, at the start of *The Great Gatsby* is also attributed to D'Invilliers, although it was actually written by Fitzgerald himself.) In Andrew

Turnbull's *Scott Fitzgerald: a Biography*, Bishop's version of his first meeting with his fellow bibliophile dryly concurs with the account in the novel. 'We talked about books: Those I had read, which were not many, those Fitzgerald had read, which were even less; those he said he had read, which were many, many more.' Above all, Bishop inspired Fitzgerald both to appreciate and to understand poetry, and, his encouragement, as well as his criticism, helped to point out directions and generally paved the way on Fitzgerald's journey towards becoming a serious writer. Four years older than his friend, his academic career interrupted by tuberculosis, Bishop was a young man with what seemed like an exotic background – his lineage included the Scottish aristocracy – and a passion for literature that the possibility of an early death from his romantic illness only served to intensify. It was a passion, moreover that Fitzgerald felt was lacking in most of Princeton's teachers.

Fitzgerald's other friend, Edmund 'Bunny' Wilson, was even harsher and unstinting than Bishop in his criticism of his young companion's cultural pretensions, sarcastically deriding his lamentable lack of learning and taste in literature. At the same time, unlike Bishop, he found himself irresistibly intrigued by Fitzgerald's undoubted talent, and fascinated that, despite his poor grammar and meager academic prowess, he could invest his prose with a vibrancy, a kind of intuitive magic that enthralled the reader. Never one to spare his friend's feelings, Wilson once famously described Fitzgerald and his talent as being similar to the tale of 'the stupid old woman with whom someone has left a diamond; she is extremely proud of the diamond and shows it to everyone who comes by, and everyone is surprised that such an ignorant old woman should possess so valuable a jewel; for in nothing does she appear so inept as in the remarks she makes about the diamond'. He then added that Fitzgerald, though quick witted and bright, 'has been given imagination without intellectual control of it … the desire for beauty without an aesthetic ideal … a gift for expression without many ideas to express'.

The shortcomings that had plagued the young Fitzgerald's first year at Newman were still present at Princeton, namely his poor grades and his inability to shine at football, the key to success and glory that forever eluded his grasp. Instead, he directed his energies towards writing, both for the stage and for the three publications generated by the college: the *Daily Princetonian*, which ran serious pieces about university life; *The Tiger*, a humorous, more obviously student-ish magazine and the *Nassau Literary Magazine*, known locally as the Lit, which featured verse, essays and stories from incipient authors. The Triangle Club, whose work had largely attracted him to Princeton in the first place, had been founded twenty years earlier by Booth Tarkington, a literary hero of Fitzgerald's when he was a boy, and it put on an annual musical show, written, composed, and performed by the students. Working feverishly, Fitzgerald wrote a musical comedy, called *Fie! Fie! Fi-Fi!* (this was later transformed into *Ha Ha Hortense* in *This Side of Paradise*), which was accepted as the 1914 production, and which became instantly successful, judged as a lively departure from the traditional vein of earlier shows – a fresher, altogether more vibrant work. He was appointed club secretary and asked to write the lyrics for the 1915 production, *The Evil Eye*. Although Edmund Wilson was writing the show's book, he grew bored of its lowbrow appeal and, happily if condescendingly, asked Fitzgerald to help him finish it, an opportunity, of course, at which his young friend leapt. Another of their friends, John Biggs, beat Fitzgerald by writing the scenario for the following year's production, *Safety First*, after the latter's contribution had been rejected, although he did write the lyrics for it. He had also started writing fiction and two of his stories were published in the Lit, which was edited by Wilson. One of these, *The Ordeal*, was of sufficient quality that a revised version was accepted by H. L. Mencken for his magazine, *The Smart Set*, five years later. Such industriousness on the literary and theatrical front could have only one result. His academic grades were woefully inadequate and he was faced with a ban on all extra-curricular activities, including The Triangle Club. This meant that he was forbidden to go on tour with them at the year's end. Despite members of the club asking the dean to relent and attempts to enlist English professors to intercede, the ban stayed and Fitzgerald was forced to cram and try to raise his grades. A severe bout of fever, which possibly led to an attack of tuberculosis (an ailment from which Fitzgerald always claimed to suffer), led to him being sent home to recuperate, with his grades still precariously low. When he returned to Princeton, he was told that he couldn't finish his junior year until his grades were sufficiently improved, and due to this academic setback, was forbidden to try for any campus office. His long-desired ascendancy to the presidency of the Triangle Club was an impossibility.

Theatrical success aside, there was another difference to the Fitzgerald who had first arrived at Princeton in 1913. This was his relationship with Ginevra King, a wealthy girl who attended Westover, and whose roommate, Marie Hersey, had invited her to spend the Christmas holidays in 1914 in Minnesota. Fitzgerald didn't actually meet her until the beginning of the following year, shortly before his return to Princeton, but she arrived heralded by rumours and legend. Within a couple of hours of meeting, they were mutually devoted, and despite their differences in wealth, background and age (he was eighteen, she only sixteen), their tryst lasted for two years. Although it might seem like nothing more than an adolescent flirtation, it was of crucial importance to Fitzgerald, emotionally and artistically, since Ginevra was fictionalized in both *This Side of Paradise* and in a number of stories, most notably as Josephine in the stories written fifteen years after they had first met, and which were eventually published as *The Basil and Josephine Stories*. Around the time that his relationship, such as it was, was on the wane, and Fitzgerald was being passed over for other, more wealthy, suitors, he overheard a remark, clearly intended for him, to the effect that boys who were poor should never consider marrying girls who were rich. Such a dismissive and haughty comment must have cut him to the quick and resurfaced in his stories and novels, notably *The Great Gatsby*, written eight or nine years later.

A romanticist and not a sensualist, Fitzgerald never really indulged in promiscuous behaviour, except during those periods of stress when he needed an intimate distraction and, possibly, some new vehicle for his emotions so that he could kick start his imagination and write about a new experience, and a new Ginevra, or Zelda. Although friends of his would venture into New York for drunken dalliances with young floozies, he rarely accompanied them, or if he did, he was enveloped in an alcoholic mist, and, as he admitted in his confessional essay, *The Crack-Up*, he 'felt each time a betrayal of a persistent idealism'. After Ginevra had been caught with her date in a rather compromising situation and been expelled from Westover, Fitzgerald's romantic idealism of her, understandably, ebbed and, as he later admitted in *The Crack-Up*, he 'hunted down the spectre of womanhood'. This remark has been interpreted by most critics as a reference to visiting a brothel, as if he was forced to take refuge in the physical once the ideal had failed him. In his excellent biography, *Some Kind of Epic Grandeur*, Matthew J. Bruccoli remarked on the use of the word 'spectre', observing that Fitzgerald, at least throughout much of his writing, seemed to equate sexual intercourse with some kind of supernatural temptation, or even corruption.

If he was romantically disappointed and academically challenged, Fitzgerald was beginning to find his feet as a writer and for a time seemed drawn to the idea of being a poet, a kind of American Rupert Brooke, and of publishing a book of poems before he was twenty-one. As he put it himself in an autobiographical piece, *Afternoon of an Author*, which was published in *Esquire* magazine in 1936 (and included in a book that appeared posthumously in 1958): 'I had only a year, and besides, war was impending. I must publish a book of startling verse before

I was engulfed.' Apart from becoming involved in a wild and fantastic plan of Monsignor Fay's to go on a secret mission to Russia in order to bring the country back into the fold of Roman Catholicism following the fall of the Czar – a bold scheme that was abandoned when the Bolsheviks assumed power – Fitzgerald continued writing verse. One poem, *The Way to Purgation*, was accepted, bought, but never actually published, by a magazine called *Poet Lore*. After returning to Princeton in the autumn, Fitzgerald received his army commission and left the university without his book of poems, and without graduating.

# The War

Fitzgerald reported to Fort Leavenworth, Kansas, for three months of basic training, but before he had left Princeton, he had shown the first draft of a novel to Fay, who regarded it with some enthusiasm, and to Christian Gauss, who was more cautious in offering his praise. Called *The Romantic Egoist*, it was a loosely constructed fictional account of his life at Princeton (which may explain Gauss' reservations). He worked on it at Fort Leavenworth, scribbling away when he should have been listening to training lectures and in the smoke-filled hubbub of the officers' club, and completed its 120,000 words on a furlough spent at Princeton. Since Fay was away in Europe, his friend Shane Leslie performed editorial duties on the manuscript, correcting its grammar and countless spelling errors before showing it to his own publisher, Charles Scribner. In an introductory letter, he described Fitzgerald as being similar to Rupert Brooke, but dealing in prose, not verse. Knowing that he was in the army and, at some point, due to go overseas to fight, and in all probability perish, Leslie coolly pointed out to Scribner that 'though Fitzgerald is still alive, it has a literary value. Of course when he is killed it will also have a commercial value.' After it was returned to Fitzgerald with suggestions made by the publisher's readers, Fitzgerald accommodated them and sent back the revised version, but it was rejected again in October, with only one of the firm's editors, Maxwell Perkins, sensing its potential and merit.

Fitzgerald was assigned to Fort Taylor, near Louisville, Kentucky, where his old friend Bishop was preparing to go overseas. As they strolled around Louisville, catching up on news of Princeton and Edmund Wilson, who was stationed in France, Fitzgerald was charmed by the beauty of both the city and its young ladies, mentally storing the scene away. When Jay Gatsby first meets Daisy Fay in *The Great Gatsby*, it is in Louisville. His unit was transferred to Camp Gordon, Georgia, and then to Camp Sheridan, Alabama, in the Deep South. Both of these places would be used in his second novel, *The Beautiful and Damned*. Hugely irresponsible as a soldier, Fitzgerald made several blunders, but also acquitted himself admirably on occasion. Whatever his military strengths or weaknesses, they all wound up as incidents in his fiction. Popular with the southern belles, he had a semi-serious relationship with one called May Steiner, who was probably cast as the sweet Dorothy Raycroft in *The Beautiful and Damned*. In the summer of 1918, when he had heard that Ginevra King was to marry an Army Air Service Officer in September, another name appears in his diary alongside those of his old flame and May: Zelda. As July becomes August, Zelda's name appears in front of May's, along with the news that he has begun revising his novel. By early September, he noted that he had fallen in love.

# Zelda

Zelda Sayre was just eighteen when she met Fitzgerald, the daughter of a judge and the youngest of five children. Although legend has it that it was love at first sight for the two of them, the diary entries would indicate that it would take a couple of months for the flames to really kindle. Hugely popular, daring and scornful of convention, conformity, reservation and the vapid emptiness of whatever was expected, she was bold, exciting and irresistible. In her only novel, the heavily autobiographical *Save Me the Waltz*, Zelda described the young, handsome Fitzgerald, immaculately attired in his Brooks Brothers uniform, strolling lightly across the dance floor, as having 'some heavenly support beneath his shoulder blades that lifted his feet from the ground in ecstatic suspension, as if he secretly enjoyed the ability to fly but was walking as a compromise to convention'. Zelda was self-confident and naturally fearless – the very opposite of her sometimes nervous and timid suitor.

Although Fitzgerald vowed to himself that he would impress her more than the other young officers with whom she flirted, even kissed, she proved elusive, maddeningly cool and tantalizing. He realized that, unlike Ginevra, whom he still thought of tenderly, this was a girl he had to keep. His charm and persistence paid off, and they started going steady. After he had flattered her and piqued her interest by telling her that she reminded him of Isabelle, the girl in his novel (who was, of course, based on Ginevra King), he gave Zelda a chapter featuring this lovely heroine, entitled *Babes in the Woods*, and, totally unused to this kind of treatment, she was immediately won over. By September, Fitzgerald was putting the word 'love' in his diary next to Zelda's name.

The following month, however, he left Alabama with his unit and went to Long Island from where they would sail to France and the war where, he believed, certain death awaited him. Glorious and romantic though this end may have been, it was not to be. While waiting to sail, the Armistice was signed and the war over. Whatever relief he may have felt, Fitzgerald was also massively disappointed. The great experience of battle was not what fate had in store for him. After leaving the girl of his dreams behind in the Deep South, after the second rejection of his novel, and after being prevented from partaking in what would surely have been an immense adventure, he was cast back into the tepid waters of a normal life, and he fragmented. Tossing everything aside, he deserted and spent a feverish few days in a self-induced purgatory of alcohol, hatred and whores. When his regiment was sent back to Camp Sheridan to await demobilization, he managed to catch up with it in Washington, meeting the troops at the station with a bottle of booze and a hooker on either side of him. His period of hedonistic despair was not entirely behind him. This act of lunacy notwithstanding, he was appointed aide to a General and assisted in dealing with civil authorities. On a visit to Montgomery, he fought with Zelda, who was possibly starting to see him without the rose-coloured field glasses of the war and wondering how far his share of dreams and promises would carry them. Around this time, in January 1919, Monsignor Fay died of pneumonia and apparently, on the day of his death, Fitzgerald felt a severe tremor grip his body, a strange incident, which seemingly never occurred to him again, but which is fictionalized in *This Side of Paradise* and elsewhere in his writing. Fitzgerald wrote to Shane Leslie, mourning their friend's death, and, ill in the base hospital with influenza himself, stated morbidly that, 'I've never wanted so much to die in all my life'. Despite this death wish, he also told Leslie that he felt 'nearly sure' that he would enter the priesthood, a fairly absurd claim from someone like Fitzgerald, who was to write, just over a year later, to the sister of an old school friend, 'You're still a Catholic but Zelda's the only God I have left now'.

# New York – Disappointment
and Failure

He was discharged on 14 February –Valentine's Day – and
went to New York, brimming with confidence that he
would make something of himself and create a life for the
two of them. The booming wartime economy was now
over, however, and jobs were scarce. Seven newspapers
turned him down, doubtless because he had no contacts,
no diploma and his only experience was in writing the
lyrics for college musicals. Shorn of the twin chaperones
of Princeton and the army, he trudged the city streets
alone, finding New York to be a harsh and hostile place far
removed from the magical realm he had encountered as a
teenager. All he could do was keep trying and keep
writing, and so he wrote everything he could to earn
some money. In *Afternoon of an Author*, he listed his
attempts at trying to make a go of it. 'I wrote movies. I
wrote song lyrics. I wrote complicated advertising
schemes. I wrote poems. I wrote sketches. I wrote jokes.
Near the end of June I sold one story for thirty dollars.'
Ironically, the story was *Babes in the Woods*, which he had
written at Princeton two years ago, and which had swept
Zelda off her feet.

Between April and June 1919, while working at a

ninety dollar a month job, writing advertising copy for the Barron Collier Advertising Agency, he also wrote nineteen stories. These received a total of 122 rejection slips that he pinned in a frieze around the wall of his rented room. Broke, he was reduced to sticking paper in his shoes where the soles had holes worn in them. His fear of poverty, of being just another figure adrift in the crowd, must have haunted him, but, always a canny and frugal writer, he recycled these lowly experiences in a story called *Dalrimple Goes Wrong*, which he sold to the *Smart Set* for forty dollars, and to infinitely greater effect in *The Great Gatsby*, written four or five years later. Intriguingly, both this story and the novel have a similar theme: a young man returning from the war, looking for work, turns to crime, using the skills learned as a soldier in order to survive and prosper as a criminal. (On a lesser note, the title of the story is often printed with the more commonplace name 'Dalrymple', although whether Fitzgerald, with his notoriously bad spelling, or the editorial department at Scribners, made a mistake is not known. Biographers, proofreaders and editors the world over, however, have followed in Dalyrimple's footsteps and gone wrong.)

In the novel, the narrator, Nick Carraway, memorably evokes a dreary bachelor existence, 'a haunting loneliness', when, in the hot mornings, he 'hurried down the white chasms of lower New York', later eating lunch 'in dark, crowded restaurants on little pig sausages and mashed potatoes and coffee'. Moments when Carraway is another one of the 'poor young clerks who loitered in front of windows waiting until it was time for a solitary restaurant dinner – young clerks in the dusk, wasting the most poignant moments of night and life' are instances when it's impossible to read Fitzgerald without feeling a pang, not for the character, but for the author. Even though he was writing this on the French Riviera, when he was already a successful author, making money, married to the girl of his dreams, he must have laid down his pen and remembered, with a sigh and a tremor in his heart, the ache and loss and loneliness of those months.

After a three-week binge, he left the city for St Paul where he rewrote his rejected novel, *The Romantic Egoist*, renamed it *This Side of Paradise*, and sent it to Scribners, where Maxwell Perkins, the one editor who had really liked its earlier incarnation, happily accepted it on 16 September, a year after its last rejection, and eight days before the author's twenty-third birthday. The poverty and feelings of failure that had haunted him in the spring were now gone and, by autumn, his luck had changed for the better. While his novel was being prepared for publication, he wrote new stories and repaired old ones, so that, by the winter, he had sold fifteen of them, sometimes to magazines that had turned them down earlier. In November, he discovered that his newly appointed agent, Harold Ober, had sold his story, *Head and Shoulders*, to the prestigious and highly selective *Saturday Evening Post* for four hundred dollars, approximately ten times that amount today. A story he wrote in eleven hours, and then rewrote and corrected in a further nine hours earned him a very cool five hundred dollars. In a mere four hours, he revised two stories that had been turned down in the previous spring and Ober sold them to the *Saturday Evening Post* for a thousand dollars. As the year drew to a close, an excited

Fitzgerald was no longer receiving rejection slips for his stories, but acceptances and increasingly substantial cheques, and in the last three months of 1919, he had earned, minus commission, eight hundred and seventy-nine dollars from writing.

# Part Two:
# 1920 – 1940

# Early Success

In January 1920, he moved to New Orleans and, having written to Zelda following the novel's acceptance, was reunited with her in Alabama, and their engagement was resumed. The following month, he returned to New York to continue his whirlwind of success, and in the 21 February issue of *The Saturday Evening Post*, his story, *Head and Shoulders*, appeared and, shortly afterwards, the film rights to it were sold. This was his first sale to the movies and his first big chunk of money. In the early part of the year, at the start of a brand new decade, Fitzgerald's income was doubling every month, and he must have felt like he had been transformed from a beggar into King Midas. Everything he touched was now turning to gold, or at least, it seemed to be, and his whole life resembled a story, a fairy tale, complete with (recaptured) princess. He had his girl back and he was becoming a successful young writer. He was selling stories for good money and he had a novel on the way.

In a wonderful series of telegrams to Zelda, he told her of each new triumph, revelling in his newfound success and wanting to share it with her. One wire in particular, about the movie sale, seems to tell at least his half of their entire story in a little over twenty words: 'I HAVE SOLD

THE MOVIE RIGHTS TO HEAD AND SHOUL-
DERS TO THE METRO COMPANY FOR TWENTY
FIVE HUNDRED DOLLARS I LOVE YOU DEAR-
EST GIRL.' It's all there – love, money (the two things
were always inextricably connected for Fitzgerald) and
success, but, with them comes also the first troubling hint
of financial dependency on his stories and, to a lesser
degree, on Hollywood, and the sense that even this
glorious and golden beginning will be tarnished. All that's
missing, in fact, are the words, 'Let's celebrate and go
crazy'. Fitzgerald spent the money, which must have
seemed like an absolute fortune (over two and a quarter
times a year's salary at the advertising agency, in fact), on a
platinum and diamond wristwatch for Zelda. He got some
mileage out of this phenomenal and touching generosity
by including the watch in his story *May Day*, where it is
an item in a shop window on Fifth Avenue.

His wedding to Zelda took place in April 1920, a week
after his novel was published, and two weeks after their
engagement was officially announced. The book was an
instant success, and within a year, had sold forty thousand
copies, not enough to make him wealthy, but nonetheless
a genuine success. His next proposed book, *The Demon
Lover*, was filleted in order to supply a few more stories
with which to pay an increasing number of bills, many of
them to bootleggers. Both the Fitzgeralds were big
drinkers, although Scott was notoriously bad at holding
his drink. Over the years, his drinking gradually descended
into full-blown alcoholism and began to affect the quality
and output of his writing, as well as his relationships with
Zelda and various friends. In the late 1930s, when

Fitzgerald was at a particularly low ebb, Arnold Gingrich, his editor at *Esquire* magazine, and certainly an ally, if not a close friend, described him as 'a real Dr Jekyll and Mr Hyde character when he had taken on board large amounts of liquor – a vicious drunk, one of the worst I have ever known'.

In 1920 this was all in the future. Fitzgerald's success, and the tremendous appeal of his and Zelda's vitality and glee caught the attention of the gossip writers in the New York magazines (presumably the same publications who had turned his stories down the previous year), and they wrote about the couple's antics endlessly. Whether they thought that it was good publicity for his career, or whether they were just being crazy, or drunk, or a mixture of all three, the couple went on a kind of madcap rampage, with Zelda diving fully clothed into the Pulitzer fountain and naked into the one on Union Square. Drunken brawls, drunken arguments and drunken parties characterised their life together as they stayed in New York, in the suburbs or away from the city. Fitzgerald was trying to write but both of them staved off boredom by partying and socializing.

Money vanished as swiftly as alcohol and Scott's intentions to work. Even this early in his career, he had set in motion a cycle from which he was destined never to escape. Writing commercial stories gave them the money to live, but prevented him from completing his next novel, and, although the novels sold fairly well, the royalties they provided weren't sufficient to finance the couple's extravagant and chaotic lifestyle. Borrowing from Scribners, or from his agent, Harold Ober, only exacerbated the problem since it reduced the sum earned when the story or novel finally did appear. Indeed, at times, he appeared to be writing in order merely to pay off a mountain of debts, rather than to live and function as an artist. In 1920, his first full year as a professional author, he had earned $18,175 – or around $182,000 in today's money – an enormous sum for a young couple to live on, and yet one that, for the Fitzgeralds, was somehow not enough.

There was an additional problem, which was nothing to do with his (or Zelda's) financial irresponsibility and bad habits, but was a conflict between commercial and artistic directions. Brilliant stories, evidence of Fitzgerald's rapidly maturing talent, often brought in very little money since they would be turned down by the high-paying *The Saturday Evening Post* and had to be sold to more literary magazines for much smaller sums. Fitzgerald was acutely and bitterly aware of this difficulty, but there was nothing he could do about it, except complain to Perkins and Ober. *May Day*, a wonderful story about the 1919 parades that resulted in clashes between socialist groups, trade unions and recently demobilized servicemen in New York, Boston and Cleveland, was turned down by *The Saturday Evening Post* and was finally sold to *The Smart Set* for a mere two hundred dollars.

Another story, the flimsy and lightweight *The Camel's Back*, was written in one twenty-four hour stint and sold to *The Saturday Evening Post* for five hundred dollars, whilst *The Diamond as Big as the Ritz*, a classic fantasy tale of wealth and hubris, ironically netted its author a fifth of the sum he was paid for a slickly concocted bit of froth called *The Popular Girl*. (It's interesting that he himself thought in monetary terms when he reviewed the troughs and wayward progress of his career, referring to his talent as having been squandered, and in the Thirties, when he found he couldn't write the kind of stories deemed acceptable by *The Saturday Evening Post*, he feared that he was 'emotionally bankrupt', a highly telling phrase, which would become something of an obsession.)

In the early 1920s, however, Fitzgerald was on the verge of becoming extremely successful, and his novel, which sold far more copies than Maxwell Perkins had dreamed it would, had brought him $6,000, a third of his income for 1920. It was followed in September by his first volume of stories, *Flappers and Philosophers*, for which he received a five hundred dollar advance and which did very well for a story collection, selling over 15,000 copies by the end of 1922. This provided Fitzgerald with some much needed capital, and all the earnings were a bonus, since he had already been paid for the stories when they appeared in magazines. Reviewing the book, H. L. Mencken, co-publisher of *The Smart Set* with George Jean Nathan, and, alongside him, one half of a critical and intellectual double act in America of the twenties and thirties, noted the schism in Fitzgerald's writing, at least in his stories, and commented on it, wondering if the writer would become a serious novelist or merely an entertainer. This was a question with which Fitzgerald himself was concerned, and which was reflected in his next novel, *The Beautiful and Damned*.

Both the novel and the stories ushered in what Fitzgerald named as the Jazz Age, which he later described memorably as 'the greatest gaudiest spree in history', and the era of the Flapper. This last was the term used to describe a modern young woman with bobbed hair, who drank, smoked and wore short skirts. The advertising blurb for the novel read, 'A NOVEL ABOUT FLAPPERS WRITTEN FOR PHILOSOPHERS', which was dreamed up by Fitzgerald and which was smartly used in the title of the story collection.

Throughout 1920, the Fitzgeralds settled into a routine of staying in various New York hotels and drinking. While Fitzgerald tried to write, Zelda, quickly tiring of her minor role as author's wife, went off with her husband's Princeton friends on a variety of excursions. He would begin to worry about what she was getting up to and would then stop writing in order to go and find her. They also rented a cottage in Westport, Connecticut, so that Fitzgerald could write, but soon invited friends from New York for drunken weekends that would usually last till Monday. On 4 July, the party was deemed to be too dull by Zelda, who summoned the fire brigade. When three fire trucks arrived and the angry fire chief asked where the fire was, Zelda allegedly pointed to her breast and exclaimed, 'Here!' Despite such bacchanalia, Fitzgerald managed to make extensive progress on his novel, which was originally called *The Beautiful Lady Without Mercy* and also *The Flight of the Rocket*, and was sometimes writing an average of five thousand words a day. A friend from Princeton, Alexander McKaig, noted in his diary that, in October, Fitzgerald had gone eight days without a drink and was working steadily. Such progress was hindered by incidents like the one in September in which a drunken Zelda, not merely threatening to leave him, actually did so and headed for the railway station, pursued by a frantic Fitzgerald, who barely succeeded in leaping aboard her train. Having recovered from this shock, the ever-practical author worked this into the novel.

They obviously effected a reconciliation, since Zelda found she was pregnant in February of the following year, forcing them to take a trip to Europe in May, before travelling became impractical. They visited England, Italy and France for two months, but were somewhat disappointed in Europe, where the fame and glamour that enveloped them in New York counted for little, and they returned to America earlier than planned. Their departure was almost jeopardised when Fitzgerald got drunk and, encouraged by a mischievous Zelda, picked a fight with a bouncer, who promptly gave him a severe beating only a few days before they were due to sail. Fitzgerald had a black eye, was festooned with cuts and bruises, had a bandaged head and no recollection of how he had earned this punishment. He wasn't too shaken to tell his friend Townsend Martin, who had tried to drag him away from the fight, that they should have been leaving that day for Europe and that Zelda had gone to postpone their crossing, which was a melodramatic untruth.

# More Success and a Dramatic Failure

After they returned from Europe, their daughter, Frances Scott Fitzgerald, or Scottie, was born in October, and the new father made a note of his wife's first remarks after giving birth, whilst she was still under the effects of ether. Her wish that her daughter would be 'a beautiful little fool' would be duly inserted three years later into *The Great Gatsby*, as Daisy Buchanan's reaction to the birth of *her* daughter.

The arrival of his second novel took somewhat longer than that of his daughter, but *The Beautiful and Damned* eventually appeared in March 1922, five or six months later than Fitzgerald had promised. Although it received largely favourable reviews, it was recognised by most critics as being a transitional work. George Jean Nathan rightly praised Fitzgerald's fairly courageous move to try and write something different, rather than another variation of the first novel, which would have been more popular and more commercially successful. As it was, *The Beautiful and Damned* sold 50,000 copies in 1922, a fairly respectable figure. Scribners had upped his royalty rate to 15% and at two dollars a copy, this netted him $15,000. Together with $7,000 for a serialization deal with *Metropolitan* magazine, $2,500 for the sale of film rights and another $3,000 or so from the sales of his second story collection, *Tales of the Jazz Age*, published in September, he should have been financially stable. But he wasn't, and he would have to churn out some more commercial stories (or 'trash', as he called them) to earn some money, if he was going to settle down and write his third novel. Hopeless with money itself, he was reasonably canny about making it, and, as an alternative to knocking out more stories, he calculated that another source of income could be the royalties from a Broadway play. He decided to write one.

Started during the early months of 1922, Fitzgerald's play was originally called *Gabriel's Trombone*, but was renamed *The Vegetable or from President to Postman*, and was a comedy and a political satire. Ironically, since it parodied the archetypal American success story (which Fitzgerald himself, to some extent, exemplified), the play was a terrible failure. Rejected by several producers throughout 1922, it was finally accepted, after lengthy revision, by Sam H. Harris. Staged at Atlantic City in November 1923, prior to its intended triumph on Broadway, it was a colossal flop and after a week was dead and buried. Published in book form by Scribners in April of that year in a print run of 7,650 copies, it didn't require another printing. Fitzgerald's 'artistic conscience', Edmund Wilson, praised it warmly, saying that it was 'marvelous – no doubt the best American comedy ever written'. Both he and its author were, however, proved wrong and Fitzgerald never bothered with the theatre again.

The failure of his play left him broke. He was forced to put off his planned attempt to write his third novel and knock out some more stories to pay his debts and give himself a cash reserve. He did this by holing up in a room above his garage and, going on the wagon at the end of the year, writing ten stories by the following March, essentially a whole collection. This superhuman effort was fuelled by pots of coffee, which caused insomnia, something he suffered from for the rest of his life. It also earned him $16,450, almost as much as he had earned in the entire year in 1920, and gave him an entire summer in which to work uninterrupted on his novel. Most of the stories were sold to *The Saturday Evening Post*, and, although they're all readable and entertaining, few are of any great merit. One of them, *Gretchen's Forty Winks*, about a commercial artist who is desperately trying to finish an important job, but is interrupted and distracted so much by his young wife that he resorts to drugging her, must have felt very close to home. Probably the best story, *The Sensible Thing*, is about a young man too poor to marry the girl he loves, and who goes off to make his fortune. This done, he returns a year later to marry her, but, though she wants him now, he knows that the magic between them has been lost. As well as being an echo (with one major difference!) of Fitzgerald's early relationship with Zelda, this is also the theme of his next novel, *The Great Gatsby*. It was one of a series of stories written between 1922 and 1924, which contain elements of the novel. *Brass Knuckles & Guitar* includes a line used in the novel and a wealthy family whose name is Katzby, and *Absolution* was originally intended as a portrayal of the boyhood of Jay Gatsby, until Fitzgerald, wisely deciding that his most famous character should remain an enigma for the reader to flesh out in his or her imagination, chose to reveal as little as possible about his background. Instead, he condensed the material into a story, which was published in H. L. Mencken's and George Jean Nathan's new magazine *American Mercury* in 1924.

# Long Island, Lardner & Liquor

Around the time that *The Vegetable* was being sniffed at by producers, Fitzgerald rented a house at Great Neck, Long Island, where he met Ring Lardner, a laconic sportswriter, humorist and fellow drinker, and the two men became friends, although Fitzgerald never got through what he called Lardner's 'noble dignity'. Lardner was a talented and extremely successful writer, who lived with his wife and four sons in a huge house, possibly the basis for Gatsby's enormous residence in the novel. Gatsby's mentor, Meyer Wolfsheim, was based on the gambler and fixer, Arnold Rothstein, the man who bribed the White Sox to throw the World Series in 1919. Lardner would have known all about that and helped Fitzgerald out with anything he needed to know. He probably also introduced Fitzgerald to a famous bootlegger called Fleischman, who may have been the basis for Gatsby, although there are others competing for this honour. Among them are the infamous bootlegger, Jack 'Legs' Diamond, who probably met Fitzgerald at a party at Great Neck, and a man called Gerlach, possibly also a bootlegger, who sent Fitzgerald a note in which he uses the term 'old sport', the phrase used by Gatsby throughout the novel. No doubt Gatsby was a composite, drawn from several real-life originals. At least

59

some of his experiences were shared with his creator.

At this time, Fitzgerald started to turn from someone who drank at parties into a heavy drinker, but one whose mood and behaviour would become erratic and often stupid when he was drunk. The heavily imbibing Lardner may have influenced him in this regard, and, although he recommended authors to his younger friend, including Dostoyevsky and Dickens, his gloomy, cynical outlook may possibly have helped to cast the shadow that hangs over Fitzgerald's exquisitely written novel. Lardner was a notorious misanthrope, and critic Clifton Fadiman believed that Lardner's talent derived from his hatred of people, stating that from such 'repulsion is born his icy satiric power'. Fitzgerald, always keen to help writers whom he liked, put Lardner in touch with Maxwell Perkins, and Scribners published seven of his story collections, the first of which, *How to Write Short Stories*, even had Fitzgerald to thank for its name. Equally, Fitzgerald must have felt highly flattered that this fellow scribe, eleven years his senior and a pathological pessimist (who, when asked to list the ten loveliest words in the English language, included 'scram', 'wretch', 'mange' and 'gangrene' among his choice), and who harboured such disdain and scorn for humanity, would actually befriend him. Some have claimed that the blonde, energetic and ebullient Fitzgerald may have seen his opposite in Lardner, a tall, balding, bulging-eyed man, and been somehow fascinated by this apparition, as if the other man represented a dark mirror image of him. Despite a huge Broadway success with his play *June Moon*, written with George Kaufman, Lardner remained despondent and continued drinking heavily, even asking Kaufman if he thought the box office sales of the play would be harmed by his suicide. He died, aged forty-eight, in 1933, when a heart attack bought on by a combination of tuberculosis and alcoholism ruled out any need for suicide. He was immortalized as Abe North, the alcoholic composer in Fitzgerald's novel, *Tender Is the Night*, although Fitzgerald had practically finished the novel by the time of Lardner's death.

# Europe Again – and Gatsby

The Fitzgeralds went to Europe again in May, 1924, after he had written a letter to Maxwell Perkins apologizing for the lack of his third novel and for his eighteen months or so of drunken laziness, but also radiating a kind of confidence, promising that the novel would be 'a consciously artistic achievement'. Almost two years earlier, in July, 1922, he had told his editor of his plans for the book: 'I want to write something *new* – something extraordinary and beautiful and simple + intricately patterned.' The work that he had done so far on the book was largely scrapped, or turned into one or two stories, and there is a sensation that he was waiting until his talent had matured sufficiently, and that now he was ready, as he explained to Perkins: 'I feel I have an enormous power in me now, more than I've ever had in a way but it works so fitfully.' He knew he was heading in the right direction, but also that he had to get it right this time, and not be distracted by parties, or friends, or the need to write a story for some ready cash. In writing this book, he was aware that he was 'thrown directly on purely creative work – not trashy imaginings as in my stories but the sustained imagination of a sincere and yet radiant world'.

Their move to Europe was based on purely financial reasons – the dollar rate was high and it would be cheaper to live there than in New York – rather than any need for a more refined cultural input. Fitzgerald's concentrated bout of story-writing meant he had $7,000, which would finance a lengthy spell of interrupted work on the novel. They went from Paris to the Riviera where, in July, while Fitzgerald worked steadily, Zelda formed an attraction to a French naval aviator called Edouard Jozan. Although little is known of how serious this was or whether the two actually slept together, Fitzgerald was utterly stunned by it and mentioned it in his personal ledger as a 'crisis'. Jozan always referred to it as merely a flirtation, but whether it was consummated or not, Fitzgerald certainly felt that 'something had happened that could never be repaired', and his faith in the marriage, and in the trust on which it depended, was shattered. Given his track record of recycling experiences in his fiction, and the fact that he had over three months between his discovery of the liaison and his completion of the novel at the end of October, it's highly likely that he included some element of his sense of hurt, disillusionment and lost faith in the book, probably in the general expression of Gatsby's own lost illusions, that reverberates throughout the text.

During this time, the couple met Gerald and Sara Murphy, an American couple who also lived on the Riviera, and who would play a prominent part in the Fitzgeralds' legend over the next ten years or so. Independently wealthy but not vastly rich, they were a gifted couple, who had left America with their three children for France in 1921. Intelligent and cultural, they had an enviable lifestyle and had succeeded in turning their whole life into a kind of impeccable and highly sophisticated art form, with their credo being an old Spanish motto: Living well is the best revenge. Gerald was a skilled artist whose infinitely detailed, abstract paintings were highly rated and later credited with anticipating the pop art style of the Sixties. Among their friends were such celebrities as the artists Pablo Picasso and Fernand Léger, the writers John Dos Passos and Archibald MacLeish and the songwriter Cole Porter. Fitzgerald immediately looked up to Murphy, seeing this stylish, well-educated, charming and civilized man as someone he would like to be. The Murphys were, initially, more taken with Zelda, since they didn't really take Fitzgerald seriously as an author and found his drinking, and drunken behavior, unseemly and unacceptable. They were, partially, to be depicted as Dick and Nicole Diver in Fitzgerald's long-gestating fourth novel, *Tender Is the Night*.

His editor, Maxwell Perkins, thought *The Great Gatsby* was of 'brilliant quality', describing it as 'an extraordinary book, suggestive of all sorts of thoughts and moods'. After Fitzgerald had finished revising and substantially rewriting portions of it, he and Zelda travelled to Capri for two months. They returned to Paris for its publication and to try and meet a young American writer, Ernest Hemingway, whom Fitzgerald had already recommended to Perkins. ('I'd look him up right away. He's the real thing.') They met in April 1925 in the Dingo bar in Montparnasse, an occasion described thirty-two years later in Hemingway's memoir, *A Moveable Feast*, where Fitzgerald, sixteen years after his death, is portrayed by his former friend as little more than an idiot and a drunken pest. The relationship between Fitzgerald and Hemingway was extremely complex and at times seemed more to resemble a rivalry than a friendship. It was further complicated by the mutual dislike between Hemingway and Zelda Fitzgerald. He thought she was mad, whilst she always regarded him as a fake, memorably describing him as 'a professional he-man', and 'a pansy with hair on his chest'.

For his part, Fitzgerald always seemed in awe of Hemingway, partly because of the latter's supposedly heroic war record (which was largely an invention), but also because of his enthusiastic participation in such manly pursuits as boxing, hunting and drinking, as well as his skill as a writer. He helped him get published by Scribners and helped him editorially with his novel *The Sun Also Rises* by suggesting extensive changes to the first thirty pages or so. Despite denying all of this in *A Moveable Feast*, Hemingway acted on his friend's advice between the manuscript and proof copies of his book and there is a ten-page letter from Fitzgerald to Hemingway documenting all of these editorial suggestions. Hemingway told Fitzgerald that Zelda was undermining him as a man and as a writer, and in one infamous incident, Fitzgerald asked his friend if he thought he was sufficiently endowed, since Zelda had accused him of being lacking in that department. On inspecting his worried friend's equipment, he pronounced it perfectly normal, but this ludicrous episode shows how unstable the combination of the three of them really was.

The Fitzgeralds didn't need Hemingway to assist them in their instability, of course, and from this point on, corrupted by alcohol, easy money and an increasingly competitive and bitter relationship, their marriage, their behaviour and Scott's literary output began to decline. In particular, he became boorish, aggressive and childish when drunk. It was only his charm and the respect garnered by his writing that made his friends, occasionally tempted to abandon him altogether, put up with him. Although she was less adversely affected by alcohol, Zelda was no better behaved and subject to violent mood swings. When they met the dancer, Isadora Duncan, Zelda grew upset by the attention she was paying her husband, and, without a word, threw herself down some stone steps. Driving home after this incident, Fitzgerald proceeded to guide their car along the tracks of a railway, where it stalled and the couple passed out. Discovered by a farmer the next morning, they were hauled off the tracks by his buggy just minutes before the first train came steaming along. When cautioned by Sara Murphy about the repetition of, and seeming need for, such extreme antics, Zelda gave a characteristically elliptical response: 'But Sara, didn't you know? We don't believe in conservation.'

Although his novel received mostly excellent reviews, it sold slowly, and most of the money it earned was already owed to Scribners and Harold Ober for advances. Fitzgerald relied on the income generated by its magazine serialization and the sale of its film and dramatic rights, and the subsequent royalties from the Broadway adaptation. Buoyed by this hefty cash bonus, a sum of approximately $25,000 (and a cool quarter of a million today), and out of debt to Scribners for the first time in four years, Fitzgerald had an ideal opportunity to work uninterrupted on his fourth novel, but instead, he wrote little during this time. He did, however, produce one of his best ever stories, a lengthy work called *The Rich Boy*, whose protagonist, Anson Hunter, was based largely on his Princeton friend, Ludlow Fowler. In this beautiful story, nearly fifty pages long, he wrote eloquently and perceptively about the people who had fascinated him since he was a child, and amongst whom he always felt an outsider, no matter how much money he made, or spent: 'Let me tell you about the very rich. They are different from you and me. They possess and enjoy early, and it does something to them, makes them soft where we are hard, and cynical where we are trustful, in a way that, unless you were born rich, it is very difficult to understand. They think, deep in their hearts, that they are better than we are because we had to discover the compensations and refuges of life for ourselves. Even when they enter deep into our world or sink below us, they still think that they are better than we are. They are different.'

It was ironic that this was written when he was comfortably off, cushioned by the box office money, and not in the usual position of having to knock out stories to pay the bills. Ring Lardner told Fitzgerald that he should have extended *The Rich Boy* and made it into a full length novel, but he demurred, saying that it was written purely as a story, a claim that was probably not true. It was included in his third collection of stories, *All the Sad Young Men*, published in 1926. This received good reviews and sold well, with its sales of more than sixteen thousand copies fetching its author almost $4,000. Like the Broadway money, this too was largely squandered as the

Fitzgeralds roamed France, drinking, fighting, making new friends, and alienating old ones. *All the Sad Young Men* was an appropriate title, since it was published in Fitzgerald's thirtieth year, and proved to be his last book for eight years, by which time, his reputation as a serious novelist was in tatters, and he was known purely as a writer of stories in the slick magazines.

The rest of their European stay consisted of more drinking, more fighting, the occasional disturbing episode from Zelda (at least one of which necessitated the application of a morphine injection), but very little writing, despite assurances from Fitzgerald to Perkins that his next novel was coming along well. In a letter written to his editor in February 1926, just days before the publication of his story collection, he wrote that TS Eliot had greatly admired and praised *The Great Gatsby*, adding 'Wait till they see the new one!', sadly unaware that this wait would be longer than he could possibly imagine. He concluded his letter with this half-joking comment about his forebears and their wayward legacy: 'Why shouldn't I go crazy? My father is a moron and my mother a neurotic, half insane with pathological nervous worry', although, again, he was unaware that it wouldn't actually be *him* that went crazy.

# America and Europe
# – Again and Again

Fitzgerald continued to be midwife to Hemingway's gestating career, and reassured Perkins and Ober that his own novel was progressing nicely. Called variously *Our Type*, *The World's Fair*, *The Boy Who Killed His Mother*, the alarmingly close to home *The Drunkard's Holiday*, *Dr Diver's Holiday* and, finally, *Tender is the Night*, Fitzgerald's problematic fourth novel suffered a long and painful birthing. As the alterations in title indicate, its themes changed along the way although, remarkably, many of the characters and much of the main theme are recognizable as those in the final version.

They returned to America at the end of 1926, having wasted at least a year, an unpleasant fact acknowledged by Fitzgerald in his ledger as he summed up the drunken, chaotic and unproductive twelve months: 'Futile, shameful useless but the $30,000 rewards of 1924 work. Self-disgust. Health gone.' Although this reveals a bitter awareness of his failings and vices, he was perhaps unable or unwilling to recognize that the riotous life they were fleeing in Europe was *their* life, the life they had chosen to live. They had left New York almost three years earlier to live and work cheaply in Europe, and now they were fleeing France for the same reasons and heading back to America, but with no clear plan for a novel on which he could work, and having wasted time and money. He would have to write some stories in order to finance their life, and these would cut into whatever progress he might make on his novel, a double disadvantage.

He was helped by an offer from Hollywood to write a comedy for Constance Talmadge, which seemed a fortuitous opportunity, but this also collapsed for a variety of reasons. Fitzgerald's script was turned down, thereby losing him an expected $12,500. The $3,500 advance had already been spent on hotel bills and the usual party-going. Whilst there, he met and was attracted to a young actress called Lois Moran, who was the cause of several scenes between him and a jealous Zelda, although she was only eighteen and their flirtation was entirely harmless. She appeared as characters in a number of stories and, more importantly, was the model for Rosemary Hoyt, the young actress in *Tender is the Night*. Fitzgerald also met Irving Thalberg, the head of production at MGM, who was acclaimed as a 'boy wonder', and who would inspire the author to create the central character, Monroe Stahr, in his final novel, *The Last Tycoon*.

They rented a house in Wilmington, Delaware, where Zelda had a burst of creativity, doubtless galvanized by her husband's admiration for the talent and success of Lois Moran. She took up ballet and resumed her writing, publishing three pieces. Often her writing was published under both of their names, partly because editors knew that his name would sell more copies of a magazine, and partly because they would be paid more if his name was on a piece, rather than just hers. Although this shared byline seemed a practical move, Zelda began to resent it, especially when their already strained marriage became increasingly competitive. Fitzgerald was now being paid $3,500 for a story, which helped them out financially, but kept him from completing any serious work on his novel.

They returned to Paris in 1928, partly for the now obsessively balletomane Zelda to study under Lubov Egorova, a former ballerina and acclaimed instructor, and partly because they were bored with Delaware and, probably, America in general. Their stay in Paris was paid for by the Basil Duke Lee stories that Fitzgerald wrote for *The Saturday Evening Post*. He wrote eight of these excellent stories, between March 1928 and February 1929, when his rate was usually six stories a year, and earned enough from them to keep afloat during this lean, but nevertheless extravagant, period. Maxwell Perkins was highly enthusiastic about the stories. Despite Fitzgerald's promise that he would send his editor the novel, two chapters at a time, Perkins was probably aware that the completed version was still fairly distant, and so urged Fitzgerald to put the Basil stories into a book. Fitzgerald refused to do so, thinking that they were about an adolescent boy and therefore not really in keeping with his standing as a serious novelist, a reputation that would soon start to diminish as the much promised novel persisted in its failure to materialize.

During this time, the Fitzgeralds led a life that was costly, not just in financial terms, but also emotionally and psychologically. Zelda accused him of having a homosexual attraction towards Hemingway and told him he was an inadequate lover. At the same time, she herself was worried that she was developing lesbian tendencies and that she was falling in love with her ballet teacher. The friendship between the two writers was severely tested and, after Fitzgerald had written a lengthy, well-intentioned and largely laudatory critique of the manuscript of *A Farewell to Arms*, Hemingway wrote 'Kiss my ass' on it. In fact, he heeded some of Fitzgerald's advice and deleted certain passages that both Fitzgerald and Perkins thought were unnecessary.

Fitzgerald wrote a handful of stories during this time, which detailed faltering and damaged marriages, and, although the fictional couples usually made good by the stories' conclusions, his and Zelda's own relationship was struggling and the bitter recriminations and mutual attacks that plagued the marriage only increased. Still, despite the corrosion caused by their marital discord, and although Fitzgerald's drinking often landed him in fights and in jail, he continued to write beautiful stories and *The Saturday Evening Post* continued to buy them – at $4,000 per story. All he had to do was keep on writing them and hope that he didn't run out of material. A further financial bonus was the $1,500 that he received in 1928 and 1929 for being a judge in a beauty contest sponsored by Woodbury soap, and a contemporary photograph shows him gazing serenely, and perhaps wistfully, at a picture of one of the entrants. Although he was doubtless happy to receive and spend the money, he was maybe aware of the irony in being asked to judge a beauty contest at a time when his wife was accusing him of homosexual leanings.

After the Wall Street Crash in October 1929, which did

little immediate *financial* damage to the couple, because they had no investments to be wiped out, Fitzgerald was grappling with his novel once again and so, in 1930, he wrote eight stories, providing $32,000, minus his agent's commissions. Five of these were stories featuring Josephine Perry, the character based on Ginevra King, the girlfriend who had turned him down, largely because he was poor. Written between April 1930 and August 1931, the five Josephine stories were accepted by *The Saturday Evening Post*, each one earning him $4,000. For a short period during this time, Fitzgerald was the highest paid short story writer in the world. How many times, when he pocketed these extremely substantial sums, must he have pondered the relatively straitened circumstances of his childhood and adolescence and reflected that the money came from his efforts to recreate, artistically, that same childhood?

# Emotional Bankruptcy
## and a Breakdown

One of these stories, *Emotional Bankruptcy*, contained a theme that was crucial to Fitzgerald over the next ten years, the idea that one had only so much emotional capital and if you spent it too quickly, then, perhaps when you needed it most, there would be nothing left. This seemed to be a warning to himself that he never heeded properly. At the same time, Zelda, still dancing obsessively and trying to write, finally revealed the strain she was under. Following a trip to North Africa to provide her with a rest, but during which they fought and she agonized over missed ballet lessons, she was admitted to Malmaison clinic, outside Paris, suffering (according to her report) from 'acute anxiety, restlessness, continually repeating "This is dreadful, this is horrible, what is going to become of me, I have to work, and I will no longer be able to, I must die, and yet I have to work. I will never be cured. Let me leave".' She was right about one thing: that she would 'never be cured', for, apart from occasional periods of lucidity, when she was allowed home, she spent much of the remainder of her life in institutions. She died in March 1948, when a fire broke out in Highland Hospital in Ashville, North Carolina, where she had been a patient, on and off, for almost twelve years. Her admission to Malmaison occurred just ten years and twenty days after her marriage to Fitzgerald.

Fitzgerald wrote a story, *The Bridal Party*, based on the wedding of Powell Fowler, brother of Ludlow Fowler, and was also promising to send his agent, Harold Ober, chapters of the novel, just as he had attempted to do so to Perkins two years earlier. Of the eight completed chapters, Fitzgerald was intending to send four, but had extensively revised one of these and had been interrupted by Zelda's breakdown. These four chapters were eventually reworked and became part of *Tender is the Night*, although the finished novel wouldn't appear for another four years. Other than Fitzgerald's drinking and increasingly chaotic working schedules, and the need to interrupt work on the novel to write the remunerative stories on which his and Zelda's livelihood depended, the main problem was that *The Great Gatsby* was a tough act to follow, and as more time went by, Fitzgerald felt that the successor would have to be the very best he was capable of. He became increasingly convinced that no less than a masterpiece would do, since one could hardly wait (at that time) five years and put out an average book.

The remainder of the year was highly traumatic. Zelda discharged herself from Malmaison and tried to return to her ballet training, but she was suffering from hallucinations that led to an attempted suicide. She was admitted to Val-Mont clinic in Glion, Switzerland, where she was diagnosed as schizophrenic, a fairly new disorder. She then entered Les Rives de Prangins clinic, near Lake Geneva. Her sister, Rosalind, blamed her illness on Fitzgerald's drinking and their chaotic lifestyle. He pointed out that the Sayre family were no strangers to mental disturbances. This was a fair comment, since Zelda's sisters were mostly neurotic, her father had suffered a nervous breakdown, her maternal grandmother had committed suicide and Zelda's brother, Anthony, was also unstable. As if to confirm Fitzgerald's diagnosis, Anthony Sayre killed himself three years later, in 1933.

The bills for Prangins were expensive, and Fitzgerald was virtually commuting between Paris and Switzerland. There was only one way to pay for it, which was writing more stories for *The Saturday Evening Post*, with the inevitable result that his novel, whilst certainly not forgotten, was put aside for months at a time. Between 1930 and 1931, he wrote seventeen stories, an impressive achievement considering his anxieties and distractions. In 1931, he earned $37,599, the highest figure until he started work in Hollywood, six years later, and out of which he had to pay the bill for Prangins, which was over $13,000. Unsurprisingly, the stories are largely about marital breakups and personal breakdowns, and several of them are very fine, with at least two of them, from 1930, ranking among his finest. *One Trip Aboard* was about a young, artistic American couple, Nelson and Nicole Kelly, who come to France to study music and painting, hoping that their lives will be culturally nourished. Needless to stay, the pair waste most of their time by excessive drinking and being indolent, and by the story's conclusion, they have both entered a Swiss clinic as patients. (Keen to be regarded by Zelda's doctor as his equal, and as an unofficial consultant on his wife's case, rather than another patient, which, in the view of some, he might well have been, Fitzgerald may have had both his characters as patients as a kind of guilty recompense to Zelda.) The story is also a stripped down version of *Tender Is the Night*, and for this reason, Fitzgerald didn't include it in any volume during his lifetime.

The second major story, *Babylon Revisited*, was written four months later and, often judged as his best, is certainly one of his most moving. An American businessman, who goes to Paris in the Twenties with his wife and daughter, falls in with a crowd of wealthy, heavy-drinking compatriots. After a drunken argument with his wife, he locks her out during a snowstorm and she perishes. Stricken with remorse and alcoholism, he gives custody of his daughter to his sister-in-law, who hates him, blaming him for her sister's death. Sober, industrious and eager to regain his daughter, his hopes to persuade his sister-in-law that he has changed and is trustworthy are squashed by the unfortunate appearance of two drunken cronies from his bibulous past. Many of the stories in 1931 are less memorable, and Ober received complaints from *The Saturday Evening Post* that the stories weren't as good as usual, and they turned down one, *Six of One*, which was bought by *Red Book* magazine for the lower price of $3,000, a disturbing indication of what was to come in the near future.

Fitzgerald's father died in the beginning of 1931 and he sailed to America to attend the funeral. A story called *On Your Own*, written in that same year, portrayed his feelings about his father's death, but through the vehicle of an actress who comes back from England to attend her father's funeral in Maryland, the scene of his own father's funeral. This character may have been based on a woman Fitzgerald met while traveling westwards to the funeral, a professional gambler called Bert Barr, who concealed her real name, the prosaic Bertha Weinberg Goldstein, beneath a cowgirl alias. He met her again in New York and later in Paris, and was quite taken with her. Though offered to various magazines, the story was never sold and eventually appeared in 1979, in a volume of uncollected stories called *The Price Was High*, although a small passage had been used earlier in *Tender is the Night*, after the death of Dick Diver's father. He also wrote an elegiac essay entitled *Echoes of the Jazz Age*, published in *Scribner's Magazine*, and later posthumously published in *The Crack-Up*, in which he eloquently mourns the loss of youth and promise, the loss of chance and, more importantly, the loss of our power to feel. It was a weakness from which he himself, perhaps, was starting to suffer.

Zelda was discharged from Prangins in September and they left Europe for America, having stayed there for four and a half years. The boat they sailed on was the *Aquitania*, the same ship that had taken them there for their first trip, ten years earlier. They were returning to America to live in Montgomery, Alabama, so that Zelda could be near her family and find peace and quiet, while Fitzgerald could, finally, finish his novel. Both of these plans were to be thwarted.

# America – Hospitals and Hollywood

Having written and sold two stories, *A Freeze-Out* and *Diagnosis*, Fitzgerald should have had time for uninterrupted work on the novel, which he was revising yet again, but, in November, he went to Hollywood to work for MGM scripting an adaptation of a novel by Katherine Brush, called *Red-Headed Woman*, a vehicle for Jean Harlow. He was reluctant to leave both the recuperating Zelda and his novel and didn't like Hollywood itself, but went because he needed the money. The initial offer of $750 a week for six weeks work was raised to $1,200, largely because Irving Thalberg had asked for him to do the job. After he started work, he quarreled with his collaborator, Marcel de Sano, and after some drinks at a Sunday party at Thalberg's house, sang an old song he'd co-written with Edmund Wilson at Princeton, which garnered him boos from some Hollywood stars and an order from the host to Charles MacArthur to take Fitzgerald home. This was all depicted in *Crazy Sunday*, written at the beginning of 1932 and one of the better stories he wrote about Hollywood. Largely about the troubled marriage of a film director and his wife, it was rejected by *The Saturday Evening Post* for being too sexually suggestive, and was published in H. L. Mencken's *American Mercury* magazine, which paid a pittance for it. Fitzgerald believed it was turned down by the other high-paying, slick magazines through the machinations of publisher William Randolph Hearst, to prevent any stars pseudonymously portrayed in it from being offended or upset.

While he was in Hollywood, Fitzgerald received loving letters from Zelda, but according to her friend, Sara Mayfield, author of a biography called *Exiles from Paradise – Zelda and Scott Fitzgerald*, she was considering the possibility of a divorce. Her father died in November 1931 and Fitzgerald worried that this bereavement might trigger a relapse. He finished the script in five weeks and returned in time for Christmas. Asked to stay and do some rewrites to his script, Fitzgerald left for Alabama instead, but felt sure that MGM would see this as him sneaking off. Whether because of this or his screenwriting deficiencies, his script was not used, and Anita Loos wrote a new one instead.

After Zelda suffered a relapse, she entered a psychiatric clinic in Baltimore, where she worked on a novel, clearly using much of the same material as Fitzgerald, i.e. their life together. Fitzgerald intended to use his Hollywood money to finance five months work on his book, but Zelda beat him to it, finishing her novel, which she called *Save Me the Waltz*, in March. She sent it to Maxwell Perkins. Fitzgerald was angry, feeling betrayed that his wife had pre-empted his use of their common material and had completed her book while he was writing stories to finance their life and, specifically, to pay her hospital bills. He also felt that Zelda, probably unintentionally, had copied sections from his work, with which she would have doubtless been familiar from its lengthy gestation. He asked her to make certain revisions and omit one or two minor details, since they would interfere with significant passages in his work. Bizarrely, one character in her book was called Amory Blaine, the name of the protagonist in his first novel, *This Side of Paradise*. After it had been revised, Zelda's novel was accepted by Perkins and would be published in the autumn. In his correspondence with his editor, Fitzgerald wrote that her novel was 'now good, improved in every way', before adding that, 'I am too close to judge it but it may be even better than I think'.

Living outside Baltimore, she recuperated and busied herself in the non-competitive pastime of painting, whilst he wrote more stories for *The Saturday Evening Post*, although the editors again complained that his stories were not reaching his usual standard. Throughout 1932, they gradually dropped his payment, down to $3,500, then $3,000, and finally, to $2,500. In the course of this year, his price had plummeted to what it was in 1925, and his earnings for the year were just under $16,000, his lowest amount since 1919, his first year as a professional author. In August, he was hospitalized, suffering from what seemed to be typhoid fever, making this the first of nine visits to Johns Hopkins Hospital between 1932 and 1937, for alcohol-related illnesses and also tuberculosis. Typically, he used this stay to fashion a story, *One Interne*, a love story about a doctor and nurse. He wrote other stories based on the hospital, although some of these must have been in poor health themselves, since he was unable to sell them. Also poor was the reception of Zelda's novel, which received disappointing reviews from critics who were baffled by some of the more overly impressionistic passages and irritated by her more grandiose descriptive ones. Blatantly autobiographical, it's the story of a couple and their troubled marriage, and it's notable that their problems are caused by both of them. In Fitzgerald's fictional depiction of their relationship, this is not always the case.

# The Depression
## – Drinking and Declining

Fitzgerald's own novel was still far from complete and he spent the autumn and winter working hard on it, planning, revising and rewriting large chunks. But he also continued to drink, imbibing on a daily basis and going on binges, although he later realised that his novel's structure and pace had suffered due to his drinking, something he admitted in a letter to Perkins. During this time, he developed an interest in politics, reading Karl Marx and drifting towards the far left. The left had begun to have an increasing influence on America's literary world, but Fitzgerald's new ideas were also in keeping with large swathes of the populace, who were turning to socialism and communism as the Great Depression continued to ravage the country.

His life with Zelda, while she spent much of her time being treated, was chaotic and fractious. He felt that while she was slowly improving, he was gradually getting worse, with this decline encompassing his health, his morale and his abilities as a writer. This idea of the cost of a wife's sanity being paid for with the well-being of her husband was central to the idea of the novel, on which he was working intensively. A transcription of a three-way discussion between Fitzgerald, Zelda and Dr Rennie, a psychiatrist from her hospital, provoked a particularly bitter quarrel, mainly over another novel that Zelda had started writing. This was about madness, and most probably centred on Nijinsky, the Russian ballet dancer who had lost his sanity and been incarcerated in an asylum. Fitzgerald was angry that, again, she was covering the same ground as him, when his own novel had been delayed, partly because he had been forced to write stories to keep them afloat. Zelda, in turn, hated being told what she could or couldn't do. Both Dr Rennie and Fitzgerald felt that allowing a mental patient to write a novel about madness was like giving a pyromaniac a box of matches, and leaving them alone in a paper mill.

Zelda decided to abandon her novel, and wrote a play called *Scandalabra*, instead. It had a one-week run in a small Baltimore theatre, but only after Fitzgerald, at her request, had cut out much extraneous material. His novel was finally nearing completion by September 1933, but needing money, he wrote three stories, which brought in $8,500. Increasingly, he was feeling that he'd used up his emotions and this was now starting to show in his writing. This was not the only thing that he'd used up. He owed Scribners, his publisher, $16,000 for advances on the novel, but hoped to recoup $30,000 to $40,000 by selling the serial rights to *Liberty* magazine. Instead, he sold them to *Scribner's Magazine* for only $10,000. He preferred this solution in some ways, because *Scribners* was a better quality magazine and he thought that, ultimately, this would be better for the book. However, it left him still in debt to his publishers, who also lent him a further $2,000, alongside the small loans from his agent, Harold Ober. These loans, borrowed at a time when his earning power was gradually being eroded by the Depression and his own diminishing confidence in his abilities, marked the beginning of his increasing spiralling into debt.

In August, a fire broke out in their house, accidentally started by Zelda burning some papers in a fireplace. (Some critics have noted that her life was punctuated by fires, and, indeed, it ended when she perished in a blaze in 1948.) A month later, Ring Lardner died, aged forty-eight, from a heart attack, probably exacerbated by alcoholism and tuberculosis. Fitzgerald was deeply saddened by his friend's death and felt that Lardner had left so much unsaid. He wrote a moving tribute to his friend in *The New Republic*, simply titled *Ring*, for which he received appreciative letters from several other writers, including Dorothy Parker, who wrote that 'it was the finest + most moving thing I have ever read'. Although he had rarely seen him since their glory days at Great Neck ten years earlier, Fitzgerald always held Lardner in the highest esteem, both as a man and a writer. Some of the grief he experienced over his friend's passing must have been because he saw, reflected in Lardner, the waste in his own life and career and the squandering of his own talent. He must have wondered about the things that he himself would leave unsaid.

As if to confirm this gloomy diagnosis, he began his visits to John Hopkins Hospital, for drying out purposes and treatment of tuberculosis-related fevers. He also took the completed typescript of his novel to Scribners for serialization, but worked on both magazine and book texts together, revising them heavily. The revisions to the serialization were so many and so substantial that it was necessary to reset the second, third and fourth installments. The serialization ran from January to April 1934 and the novel was finally published on 12 April, exactly nine years and two days after the publication of *The Great Gatsby*.

Two months before the book was published, Zelda was again hospitalized and, in May, was sent to a hospital outside Baltimore in a catatonic state. While he fretted over the reception and sales of his novel, Fitzgerald also resigned himself to the harrowing fact that she would never completely recover and they would never be able to have a life together again. In his *Notebooks*, he recorded his reaction to this realization: 'I left my capacity for hoping on the little roads that led to Zelda's sanitarium.' After his novel was published, he dropped his rule of forbidding Zelda from writing and even tried to get Scribners to publish a collection of her stories and essays. Both of them spent some time polishing and editing various pieces, but the project foundered.

Fitzgerald's novel met with a generally favourable response, although even the good reviews were tempered with criticisms of the novel's unevenness and its lack of unity. Some of the critics who liked it found it somewhat disappointing, largely because its lengthy delay, and Fitzgerald's own reputation, had created a sense of anticipation that was unrealistic, even unhealthy, and that could only lead to a feeling of anticlimax. There was also a kind of incredulity, where critics found it difficult to reconcile Fitzgerald's attempts to be a serious novelist with the commercial slickness of his magazine stories, and his overall image of bon viveur and man about many towns. Admirably, and realistically, Fitzgerald himself summed up the difficulties with the novel's structure and momentum: 'The man who started the novel is not the man who finished it.' The problems with its structure led to Fitzgerald revising it. In an edition published posthumously in 1951, the events of the book followed in chronological order, and not as originally written. However, the 1934 non-chronological version is usually considered the definitive text, and certainly it has much more dramatic impact.

Fitzgerald's rivalry with Hemingway meant that he was keen to see what the other writer thought of the novel, and he wrote to him asking him for his opinion, asking him to, 'For God's sake drop me a line and tell me one way or another. You can't hurt my feelings.' Hemingway included something of a lecture in his faintish praise, to which Fitzgerald responded in a dignified, but defiant, manner. The following year, however, Hemingway wrote to Maxwell Perkins and candidly admitted that the novel 'gets better and better', adding later that he found it 'amazing how good much of it is', before finally admitting that 'much of it was so good it was frightening'.

# Debts and Despair

The novel's sales were not going to drag Fitzgerald from his deepening debt, so he started writing stories, beginning a series of historical tales set in ninth century France and featuring a character called Philippe, which he hoped to expand into a whole book. He sold four of the stories to the *Redbook* magazine, for between $1,250 and $1,500 each, but they were written while he was drinking and were some of his shoddiest work, and the projected book never materialised. Other stories were sold to *The Saturday Evening Post* for $3,000 each, but the editors stressed that these stories were bought with reluctance and were not what they really wanted from Fitzgerald. He also began selling stories to a new magazine called *Esquire*, whose editor, Arnold Gingrich, bought material from Fitzgerald and helped him until the author's death. *Esquire*'s prize contributor was Hemingway but, even so, as a publication that started in the Depression, the magazine couldn't afford to pay Fitzgerald more than $250 a piece. He regarded anything he gave them as emergency material but he still tested Gingrich's patience and support by asking them for advances.

During this time, although busy, he was often engaged in work that was either rejected or that he scrapped himself. He was wasting time and energy on material that generated no money, whilst continuing to borrow from Scribners. Eventually Maxwell Perkins stopped lending him any more, forcing him, not for the first time, to borrow money from his mother, which he found galling and humiliating. His agent, Harold Ober, told him that he was seriously endangering his marketability as a commercial author by his increasing unreliability and also by his stupid tendency to attempt negotiating with editors when drunk. The most decent work he did in this increasingly fraught period was assembling his fourth collection of stories, *Taps at Reveille*, which was published in March 1935, and received good reviews, but sold relatively poorly, largely because spending $2.50 on a volumes of stories was something of an indulgence during the Depression. The book contained eighteen stories out of a possible fifty and, although Fitzgerald had various schemes for collecting other work into two or three volumes, including the Basil and Josephine stories, a volume of recent stories and a non-fiction collection, none of these emerged, at least not during his lifetime. The book was dedicated, perhaps hopefully, to his agent, Harold Ober, who had been advancing Fitzgerald large and small sums for over fifteen years, and continued to do so until 1939.

1935 rolled on and Zelda continued to be seriously disturbed, making several attempts at suicide. Fitzgerald grew anxious about his own welfare, particularly the health of his lungs and his general feelings of despair as his debts mounted and his ability, and the opportunity, to earn money receded. During this period, he corresponded with Zelda, tried to write stories, drank, was diagnosed as suffering from tuberculosis and had an affair with a wealthy Texan woman called Beatrice Dance. Terminating this affair in a letter, he also included a very needy letter from Zelda, as if to convince Beatrice that things were over and that he could never leave his wife, whom he sneakily, but not without some truth, called 'my invalid'.

He managed to sell seven stories during this difficult year, but writing them was increasingly hard and none of them was significant. The days when he laboured conscientiously for hours over what he grandly dismissed as trash, and for which he was handsomely paid, were long gone. He was now trying to pay immediate bills – living expenses – and worry about the large debts at a later date. To do this, he was rushing through stories, sending off rough drafts to editors in the hope that his name and dwindling reputation would do the trick. Increasingly, it didn't, and now he really was knocking out hack work, as opposed to the commercial work that he had so loftily disparaged. He was desperately hunting for inspiration, looking for some emotional reservoir that would get the juices flowing again. He started writing a series of stories about a girl called Gwen, a teenager with a widower father. Gwen was based on his daughter, Scottie, and the model for the father was only too clear. Obviously written with the successful Basil and Josephine stories in mind, two out of the four Gwen stories were bought by *The Saturday Evening Post*, but the others were rejected and the magazine advised him to drop the series. The other two were bought, but not actually published, by the *Pictorial Review*. One of these, *Make Yourself at Home*, was resold in 1939 to Liberty, appearing as *Strange Sanctuary*, a rather apt title. In the increasingly bleak period from 1935–7, there were numerous stories that remained unsold, and one, *I'd Die for You*, was rejected by seven different publications, ranging from *The Saturday Evening Post* to *Woman's Home Companion*. When he wasn't writing these inferior stories, he was drinking and being hospitalized for lung problems and to dry out.

# The Crack-Up

At the end of the year, he left Baltimore for North Carolina, living in a cheap hotel, doing his own washing and eating tinned food. Desperate for funds, he sent Arnold Gingrich, at *Esquire* magazine, an article, since Gingrich had promised to wire him some money, but needed something to show the accountants. What he got was a confessional piece entitled *The Crack-Up*, which was followed by two others: *Pasting It Together* and *Handle with Care*. Although contemporary opinion was divided about them, they became his best-known non-fiction work. Nobody but Fitzgerald could have written so clearly and imaginatively about not being able to write. Almost unbearably ironic, the essays provide a perfect example of his theory of emotional bankruptcy, underlining the fact that, having used up his capacity for feeling about people and about life itself, he could no longer write about them. Inevitably, this public exposure of his faults and weaknesses resulted in Fitzgerald becoming even more uncommercial, since editors had it straight from the horse's mouth, as it were, that he had lost his ability to write. Some people thought he was wallowing in his failure, and Maxwell Perkins found the articles an embarrassing mistake. Hemingway, then at his commercial peak, thought they were a lowly act of cowardice. They did generate considerable interest, however, and there was a possibility of a book of autobiographical pieces but, in the end, nothing came of it.

Possibly due to his and Zelda's extensive experience of hospitals, he wrote two stories about a nurse whose nickname was 'Trouble', but *The Saturday Evening Post*, after reluctantly buying one, rejected the other, advising him to drop this character and come up with a new one. This was the last of the sixty-five Fitzgerald stories that they bought, so that his most lucrative market was now closed to him. Bad luck plagued him. Zelda was now beset with religious mania and was moved to another hospital, where the minimum fee was $240 a month, while Scottie was accepted in a school where the fees were $2,200 a year. In July he broke his right shoulder diving and then fell in the bathroom while his arm was in a cast, developing arthritis in his bad shoulder, as he lay, immobile, on the bathroom floor. In August, his mother died and, still in a cast, he was unable to attend her funeral. Feeling guilty over his poor fulfillment of his duties as a son, he was, however, relieved when his share of the estate temporarily improved his finances, but the bequest of nearly $23,000 was soon whittled down by his debts and he was left with around $5,000. As if this wasn't bad enough, his old pal Hemingway published a story, *The Snows of Kilimanjaro*, in *Esquire*, about a writer who is dying and who surrenders his dignity, which openly mocked Fitzgerald and used his name. Stung by this, he sent a dignified reply asking his erstwhile friend if he would, 'Please lay off me in print'. Hemingway's response to this, now lost, was described by editor Arnold Gingrich as 'brutal', whilst Maxwell Perkins considered Hemingway's slur to be 'contemptible'. When the story appeared in a book, the name was changed, at Fitzgerald's request. Hemingway merely wanted it altered to 'Scott', hardly a conciliatory gesture on his part, but, after the intervention of Perkins, it was changed to the more anonymous 'Julian'. Unfortunately, appearing in the same issue of the magazine was Fitzgerald's own piece, *Afternoon of an Author*, another confessional essay, which though brilliantly written, was exactly the sort of thing that Hemingway felt justified his barbed criticisms.

Fitzgerald did himself no favours, however, and an ill-timed interview with the *New York Post*, conducted when he was both ill and drinking, revealed him in an utterly awful light, portraying him as nothing more than a drunk, his face bearing 'the pitiful expression of a cruelly beaten child'. Fitzgerald was so appalled at seeing the article that he took an overdose of morphine which, fortunately, he vomited back up. Descending into the kind of twilight existence that might have been the province of a character in a pulp magazine, he was refused admission to his hotel unless accompanied by a nurse after he had fired a revolver in another suicide bid. At a dance given for his daughter, he got drunk and told her guests to leave. The father of Scottie's friend took the two girls home, and Fitzgerald, after the dance was finished, paid the band to continue playing, whilst he sat on his own with only a bottle of gin for company. He spent the Christmas period in hospital, recovering from influenza and drying out.

With his earnings plummeting to just over $10,000 in 1936, he continued to try and write stories that would earn him some decent money, but failed to do so. Instead, he sold five stories to *Esquire*, most of which were fairly poor. One, however, *Financing Finnegan*, was very good. A wryly humorous account of a writer who was 'the perennial man of promise in American letters', but who keeps getting bailed out by his publisher and agent, it was a kind of apology to and rueful private joke for the benefit of Maxwell Perkins and Harold Ober. It was turned down by *The Saturday Evening Post* on the grounds that not enough people would be interested in it, an odd bit of reasoning given the stir caused by *The Crack-Up* articles, and was sold to *Esquire* for the usual $250. Fitzgerald sold one other piece in this period, *Early Success*, an excellently written account of his golden days, which was bought by a magazine called *American Cavalcade*. Along with *Financing Finnegan*, it was the best of his writing from this traumatic time and, in a sense, the two pieces act poignantly as bookends to his career so far. *Financing Finnegan* concludes memorably with the line, 'But the movies are interested in him – if they can get a good look at him first and I have every reason to think that he will come through. He'd better.' In July of 1937, that's exactly what Fitzgerald did. He went to Hollywood, where MGM had hired him for six months at $1,000 a week.

# Hollywood (Again)

This was the third time that Fitzgerald had tried to make a success in Hollywood, and he knew that it was his last chance to make it and also to pay back his massive debts. He owed Harold Ober just over $12,500, at least $9,000 to Scribners and $1,100 to Maxwell Perkins. He had chipped away at his life insurance policy until it was worth only $30,000 instead of its original value of $60,000 and was behind in Zelda's hospital payments which, in 1938, were $6,780 a year. At one point, he stated that he actually owed $40,000 when he went to Hollywood, a sum that may not have been an exaggeration. Calculating how much of his salary would be allotted to cover the various sums owed, he foolishly reckoned that he would have honoured all of his debts within a year. He paid back Ober and Perkins their money by the end of 1938, but by the time of his death two years later, he still owed Scribners over $5,000.

He knew that he'd be working for Hollywood's best studio and, if his option was renewed, he would be earning at least $1,000 a week for another year, but the work was just not what he wanted to do, and the way the studio's work schedule was arranged was tough, since he slept badly and was usually tired in the daytime. On the wagon, he drank bottles of Coke, sometimes as many as twelve per day, and he lined up the empty bottles around his office walls until they formed a complete rectangle. In order to sleep, he took two Nembutals a night, along with three teaspoons of chloral. In order to feel awake in the morning, he took Benzedrine. When his heart began to trouble him, he added Digitalin to his nocturnal pharmacological input.

He was shy and self-effacing and seemed chronically sensitive to the fact that he had taken a wrong step and that his glory days were behind him. He also seemed embarrassed and ashamed to be working in Hollywood, and usually refrained from sitting at the writers' table in the studio commissary, where he could have lunched and laughed with such scribes as Dorothy Parker, S. J. Perelman, George Oppenheimer and Ogden Nash. Sometimes, he would sit at another table, having lunch with Anita Loos and Aldous Huxley, and actors Spencer Tracy and Clark Gable, but he was quiet, and rarely contributed to the witty repartee. Doubtless, he felt alienated, not just because he was an Easterner in California, or a novelist working on a mere movie script, but because he was a heavy drinker who was on the wagon, and often surrounded by other heavy drinkers, who weren't. Always used to being the center of attention, he felt as if he'd been exiled and forgotten, so much so that he actually wrote a postcard to himself: 'Dear Scott – How are you? Have been meaning to come in and see you', and signed it, 'Yours Scott Fitzgerald'.

# Sheilah Graham – A New Romance

When he had only been there a short while, he met an Englishwoman, a columnist called Sheilah Graham, at a party thrown by writer Robert Benchley to celebrate her engagement to the Marquess of Donegall. Although he didn't actually talk to her, he recognized her resemblance to Zelda when she was young, and met her properly at another party a few days later, after the Marquess had returned to England. Like a scene from one of his stories in *The Saturday Evening Post*, his first words to her were 'I like you', to which she replied 'I like you, too'. Two days later, they met again and danced for much of the evening. She knew he was a writer, but had no knowledge of his work, nor, importantly, of his illustrious past. She thought him witty and attentive and saw how respectfully his friends treated him, but was confused by some of his quirks. At a dinner with his daughter Scottie and some of her friends, she was puzzled to see this charming man change into a bossy father who badgered his daughter throughout the evening. Afterwards, she sympathized with this paternal stress and, not wanting him to leave, invited him into her house. According to her rather misty-eyed account in *Beloved Infidel*, the book she wrote with Gerold Frank, she whispered '"Please don't go, come in", and I drew him in and as he came in he kissed me and suddenly he was not a father any more and it was as though this was as it should be, must be, inevitable and foreordained'.

What was certainly 'inevitable' was that Fitzgerald, perhaps instinctively sniffing out a story, became obsessed with discovering her past, since her airy tale of coming from an upper-class English family and being a chorus girl before becoming a journalist was entirely fictitious. Born Lily Sheil in a slum in East London, she was mostly raised in an orphanage. At eighteen, she married a much older man, who had no money but taught her manners and how to speak properly. Slowly making her way through London society, she came to America to be a journalist in 1937, by which time her marriage was over. Rattled by Fitzgerald's relentless curiosity about her past, she wept and revealed the truth, only to be amazed by his interest in her noble attempts to better herself and his offer to educate her. Her confession that she had slept with eight men shocked the rather puritanical author and, since he was on the wagon, she had no idea what any of this information would mean to him when he was drunk and raving.

She found out soon enough, since Fitzgerald tumbled off the wagon in October, jealously getting drunk after she was late calling him, following a dinner with writer Arthur Kober. Having broken her engagement to the Marquess of Donegall, she was now more seriously involved with Fitzgerald, and her awareness that he was an alcoholic triggered off unpleasant, youthful memories of East End drunks. Having struggled to escape her lowly beginnings, she also anxiously pondered the wisdom of jeopardising her new career by consorting with another drunkard. Curiously, at this period, Fitzgerald heard from his first love, Ginevra King, who was in California, and they met for the first time in nineteen years. Nervous and in need of Dutch courage, he drank too much and they never met again. During this time, he worked on the screenplay for *Three Comrades*, based on a novel by Erich Maria Remarque, author of the World War I classic *All Quiet on the Western Front*, and received his only screenplay credit, which was, to his chagrin, shared. The film was a huge smash, however, and, in spite of his problems with the script and the shared credit, he was rewarded with a renewal of his contract and a raise to $1,250 a week for the next year.

Such success didn't last long since Fitzgerald disgraced himself on a trip to Chicago with Sheilah, where she was trying out for a weekly radio talk show. Drunk, he caused trouble at the studio by trying to take over and by punching the show's sponsor, before being thrown out. After drying out back in California, he started work on a script for Joan Crawford entitled *Infidelity*, but was stymied by the subject matter. As MGM was noted as a studio that made family films, the purchase of a story about marital unfaithfulness was an unwise decision. Fitzgerald's script of 104 pages necessarily lacked an ending, since there was only one way it could logically end. (What he felt as a husband to a distant, ailing wife about writing on such a topic, when he was himself having an affair, has never really been recorded.) Despite suggestions that the film be re-titled *Fidelity*, the project was dropped, much to Fitzgerald's disappointment.

His relationship with Sheilah continued, and though he made no secret of it, letting her meet the Murphys, Maxwell Perkins, Harold Ober and Edmund Wilson, as well as Scottie, who liked her, he was troubled by its 'illicit' nature and the necessity of keeping it a secret from Zelda and her family. His feelings about Sheilah and her previous lovers caused him unrest. They both provoked him into heavy drinking and were exacerbated by it. Sheilah discovered, after his death, that on the back of a photograph of her, he had scrawled, obviously when drunk, 'Portrait of a Prostitute'. Although this seems horrendous, it's worth remembering that Fitzgerald was, when on the wagon, working hard at a job he hated, paying off his collection of debts, keeping Zelda in an expensive hospital and sending Scottie to Vassar, as well as paying for a trip to Europe and regular trips to California for her. He was, in effect, a working single parent, one who was beset with ill health and worries, and so perhaps should not be entirely blamed for what was, at times, atrociously callous behaviour.

Whilst he was engaged in screen work, Fitzgerald wrote nothing for any magazines, but probably began planning a Hollywood novel around 1938. *This Side of Paradise* was now out of print, and he was worried that he would be forgotten as a novelist. His contract with MGM was not renewed, and his last job for them was working on a treatment for *Madame Curie*, which had originally been scripted by Aldous Huxley. After he had earned around $85,000, he was dropped at the end of January 1939, his last work being a revision of part of the script for David O. Selznick's *Gone With the Wind*. His instructions were that his revisions could only use dialogue that was already present in Margaret Mitchell's blockbuster novel. He worked on the script for two or three weeks as just one of a team of sixteen writers. This system of using multiple writers on a script was one of the main things that he hated, as a writer, about the studios' method of developing screenplays.

# Drinking, Sobriety
and The Last Tycoon

When he wasn't working or drinking, Fitzgerald enjoyed a quiet, pleasant time with Sheilah, helping to give her an all round education with a syllabus he devised and which he called the 'College of One'. He also attended small parties given by humorist S. J. Perelman and his brother-in-law, Nathanael West. He admired West, who earned money from B-movie scripts so he could write novels that were critically acclaimed, but that sold poorly. Fitzgerald also tried to offer his services to studios as a freelance writer and did piecemeal work to pay a few bills. One important job was co-writing the script for a film called *Winter Carnival*, produced by Walter Wanger for United Artists. He would be collaborating with Budd Schulberg, a recent graduate from Dartmouth, who was the son of Paramount executive B. P. Schulberg, and who had written the original script that they would be working on. Fitzgerald spent much of his time grilling Budd about his father and the inside track of studio business, and was sure that he could turn his findings into material in his Hollywood novel.

Since they had written only a few pages, Wanger insisted they accompany the crew to Dartmouth to pick up atmosphere and inspire them. B. P. Schulberg's gift of champagne for their flight to Dartmouth set Fitzgerald off on a bender which lasted the whole of the three-day trip and resulted in him being fired, catching a severe cold and finally being hospitalized in New York. Schulberg, who was also fired, was rehired by Wanger and finished the script alone. He also turned the incident into the basis for a novel entitled *The Disenchanted*, in which the protagonist is a once glamorous, drunken writer called Manley Halliday, clearly based on Fitzgerald, despite Schulberg's claim that he was a composite of various Hollywood writers.

Freed of the responsibility of turning up for work each day Fitzgerald drank freely, engaging in violent arguments with Sheilah, who tired of his dreadful behaviour. After they fought when she tried to wrest a revolver from him (a pitiful echo of his suicidal period of three years earlier), she had had enough and told him 'Shoot yourself, you son of a bitch!'. Rather than pulling the trigger, he went instead to see Zelda, taking her to Cuba, where she stayed in the hotel praying and he roamed Havana, drinking and getting into a fight. Returning to New York, he continued drinking, and was eventually hospitalized. This unfortunate and shambolic episode was the last time he saw his wife, although they corresponded warmly and frequently. Returning to California, he miraculously made it up with Sheilah and began writing stories again, most of which were rejected.

A request to borrow money from Ober was regretfully declined and an astonished and angry Fitzgerald wrote several letters before breaking with his agent permanently.

Although Ober continued to act as Scottie's guardian and was proud to do so, he was in a severe quandary about her father. In the end he stuck to his decision, and, no doubt wisely, didn't lend Fitzgerald any more money. For the remainder of 1939 and all of 1940, Fitzgerald acted as his own agent, and continued writing stories that were largely unsold, working on his novel, and doing very occasional script work. His main source of income was from selling stories to *Esquire*, where Arnold Gingrich bought seventeen tales about a boozy hack writer and rogue called Pat Hobby, who had once earned good money writing intertitles in the days of silent movies. Fitzgerald carefully avoided duplicating any of this material in his proposed Hollywood novel, and these amusing, but cynical stories, which largely detailed the unscrupulous Hobby's misadventures and scams to raise a few dollars, helped to keep *The Last Tycoon* free from any harshness and weariness. One fine, non-Hobby story, *Last Kiss*, was rejected by *Cosmopolitan* and *Collier's*, but is a kind of forerunner to the novel, in that the heroine, an English actress, like *The Last Tycoon* character, Kathleen, is based on Sheilah Graham. Unpublished at the time of his death, it appeared in *Collier's* in 1949, and the magazine paid $1,800 for it. To add to this irony, it also earned $1,000 as a bonus for being that issue's best story. Unfortunately, the author was no longer alive to spend it.

Throughout 1940, Fitzgerald worked hard on the novel, assisted by a secretary, Frances Kroll, whose tasks ranged from typing out his manuscripts, sending flowers to Sheilah after a quarrel and removing empty gin bottles. After going on the wagon and staying on it, he also did occasional film work, including a script based on his wonderful story *Babylon Revisited*, the film rights of which had been bought for $1,000 by Leslie Cowan, an independent producer, who also hired Fitzgerald to write the screenplay at $500 a week. These were paltry sums but, although this kept him from working on the novel, it gave him $5,000 and bought him time to write in long, uninterrupted bursts. His film work finished after Twentieth Century Fox hired him to write a script based on Emlyn Williams' play, *The Light of Heart*, which was about, of all things, an alcoholic actor. It paid $1,000 a week but, after he had done three revisions, his script was deemed too gloomy. Given the subject matter, this was hardly surprising.

This finished in mid-October and then he was free to work on his novel in the nine weeks or so that remained of his life. In a letter to Zelda, a few days after he'd completed his script duties for Fox, he wrote that he was 'deep in the novel, living in it, and it makes me happy'. A week or so later, he told her that it was hard work, but he expected this: 'I feel people so less intently than I did once that this is harder. It means welding together hundreds of stray impressions and incidents to form the fabric of entire personalities.' A few weeks later, he wrote, self-mockingly, of how the book was shaping up and of the actual rate of progress: 'It will, at any rate, be nothing like anything else as I'm digging it out of myself like radium – one ounce to the cubic ton of rejected ideas.'

Such digging must have taken its toll, since at the end of November, Fitzgerald suffered a heart attack while he was in Schwab's drugstore. Resting and recuperating at home, writing a couple of hours a day using a board, he continued with his book. He wrote to Zelda in December, saying that he thought that his 'heart is repairing itself but it is a gradual process that will take some months'. He planned to have the first draft of his book finished by 15 January. A dizzy spell and trouble walking to his car occurred on 20 December, but he was expecting a visit from his doctor the next day. Before the doctor arrived, Fitzgerald was dead. He had been sitting by the fireplace reading a Princeton alumni magazine when he stood up, reached out to the chimney, then collapsed. Eyes shut, he lay on the floor, having died of coronary occlusion at 5.15 pm, 21 December 1940, according to the coroner's report. He was forty-four years old and he had written 44,000 words of his final novel.

# Aftermath

He was buried on 27 December in the Rockville Union Cemetery, Maryland, in a funeral that was similar to Jay Gatsby's. There were thirty friends and relatives, including Scottie, the Murphys, Maxwell Perkins and his family, Harold Ober and his, and some friends from Princeton and Baltimore, but not Zelda, who was unwell. Sheilah felt it best that she didn't attend. Fitzgerald left behind more debts, although he had paid off the bulk of them, but still owed over $4,000 to Zelda's hospital, almost $5,500 to Scribners and smaller sums to Perkins and Ober. Perkins was adamant about publishing Fitzgerald's unfinished novel, if only to earn some money for the estate, and offered it to one or two writers to complete it. Budd Schulberg and John O'Hara both refused, saying that no one could add to Fitzgerald's writing. Finally, it was published as it was, edited by Edmund Wilson, together with *The Great Gatsby* and five of Fitzgerald's best stories. The novel, as far as it went, drew respectful and favourable reviews all tinged with sadness over the loss to American letters. The one notable exception was Hemingway, who dismissed it as being stale fare, with the novel's plan bolstered by 'impossible dramatic tricks'. Perkins had considered Hemingway as a possible contender to complete the book, but Zelda vetoed the idea.

Zelda lived until 1948 when a fire, one of the many that occurred through her life, burnt part of Highland hospital, killing nine patients, including her. Identified only by the scorched remnant of a ballet slipper found under her corpse, she was buried with Scott, until both were re-interred in the Fitzgerald family plot in 1975. Before she died, what has been described as 'the Fitzgerald revival', had started with the publication in 1945 of *The Crack-Up*, consisting of autobiographical pieces, letters and selections from his notebooks. Also published that year was *The Portable F Scott Fitzgerald*, edited by Dorothy Parker. Within a few years, this revival had become a rebirth, with millions of copies of his books selling to new generations. Taught in classrooms, translated into over thirty languages around the globe, his books are more popular than ever, with his finest, *The Great Gatsby*, selling over 300,000 copies annually in America alone. If it's undeniably tragic that Fitzgerald never lived to see or enjoy this success, then what he said was true: 'Show me a hero and I will write you a tragedy.'

# Part Three:
# Fitzgerald's Works

# The Novels

## *This Side of Paradise*, New York, Scribners, 1920.

Published in 1920, Fitzgerald's debut is the story of young Amory Blaine, a privileged, lazy and self-interested Princeton student. Written and rewritten while Fitzgerald was in the army and at his parents' house in St Paul, Minnesota, the novel was originally called *The Romantic Egoist*, the title eventually given to the book's first section, but it was renamed when Fitzgerald borrowed a line from a Rupert Brooke poem, *Tiare Tahiti*. Extremely autobiographical, the novel is a delightful concoction that wears its influences – H. G. Wells, Compton Mackenzie – on both sleeves, but also has a lot of Fitzgerald's own character and life, with much of the early material taken from his diaries. After an interlude from May 1917 to February 1919, which presumably covers Amory's military career, but which Fitzgerald, not having gone to Europe in the war, wisely decided not to write about, there follows the second section of the book, *The Education of a Personage*. This concerns itself with Amory's (and Fitzgerald's) life after the war and includes the death of his mentor, Monsignor Darcy; a potentially disastrous bender in New

York, which is accompanied by a strange and somewhat clumsy supernatural episode; his faltering career as an advertising copywriter, and his break up with the girl of his dreams, Rosalind, who was partly based on Zelda and shared the name of her sister. An extremely impressive success when it was first published, selling out its initial print run of 3,000 in a few days, and going on to sell over 40,000 copies, the novel made its author a celebrity overnight and launched his career in a spectacular fashion.

## The Beautiful and Damned, New York, Scribners, 1922.

Fitzgerald's second novel appeared in 1922 and marked a transitional phase in his career. Written in 1920 and 1921, it shows the influence of the critic H. L. Mencken. It is the story of a young couple, Anthony and Gloria Patch, who are wealthy but, due to a seemingly trivial, if unfortunate incident, are deprived of the bulk of their riches by Anthony's stern and capricious grandfather. Their marriage, once destined to be a golden, glamorous union, descends into an inferno of drinking, bickering and bitterness. With the outbreak of war, Anthony enlists and is stationed in the South, where he engages in what he assumes is a harmless flirtation, before returning home at the end of the hostilities and attempting to contest his grandfather's will and salvage his marriage, his riches and his life.

The Fitzgeralds' own drinking and his and Zelda's chaotic lifestyle meant that he had to revise the novel extensively after their trip to Europe in 1921. Although the finished book was inconsistent, it was brilliant in parts. Anthony's service in the army during the war and his flirtation, or tryst, with a young Southern belle named Dot, is a powerful section, but doesn't really fit in with the rest of the book, and its general patchwork effect confused and disappointed some critics. Others saw it as a brave sign of progress on the part of a young writer who, for commercial reasons, could have simply opted for rehashing his debut. Edmund Wilson, always a rather overbearing critic of his friend's work, accurately summed up the book's haphazard impact in a letter when he was reading the manuscript: '... though I thought it was rather silly at first, I find it developing a genuine emotional power which he has scarcely displayed before'. The novel sold almost the same amount as its predecessor, but proved to be a significant stepping-stone to Fitzgerald's masterpiece.

## *The Great Gatsby*, New York Scribners, 1925.

Published in 1925, this slender novel has rightly been hailed as the most perfect American novel of the 20th century. One of the most romantic of modern love stories, set in the bootleg liquor–fuelled roaring twenties, it's also a very dark tale that depicts the contrast between the slick, cynical East and the provincial Midwest. Alongside this it's also a razor sharp satire on the rags-to-riches myth of American self-improvement, with its exquisitely honed prose unmasking the nightmare lurking at the core of the American Dream. Millionaire Jay Gatsby, host of the fabulous, legendary parties that enliven the small community at Long Island, is a mystery, an enigma. Where did he come from? How did he earn his money? Was he a spy? Was it true that, as some believed, he had killed a man? Only his neighbour, the book's amiable narrator, Nick Carraway, is privy to some of Gatsby's secrets and even he remains unsure. As the immaculately fashioned plot unfolds, tantalising glimpses of Gatsby's past are revealed, showing a man whose meteoric rise to wealth and power is fuelled by his obsessive love for the beautiful Daisy Buchanan. Daisy is Nick's cousin, a young married woman with 'a voice … full of money', who is caught between her still incandescent old flame and her husband Tom, a wealthy, bullying womaniser. Inexorably, the narrative races towards a shocking and tragic conclusion.

With perfect ease, Fitzgerald captures the America, and specifically New York, of the 1920s, when life was lived at a faster, more frantic pace and anyone could do anything they wanted, as long as they had a little cash, took just another sip … His masterpiece, written when he was just twenty-eight, continues to live on, as mesmerising now as it was when it first appeared, a unique and dazzling jewel, and one that Maxwell Perkins thought 'an extraordinary book, suggestive of all sorts of thoughts and moods'. Perkins added one comment, which has struck everyone who has read the novel, and which surely must account for its endless and concentrated power: 'It seems in reading a much shorter book than it is, but it carries the mind through a series of experiences that one would think would require a book of three times its length.' Ironically, for a novel that concerns itself with wealth, its author, already owing $6,000 to his publishers in advances, requested a lower royalty rate for *The Great Gatsby* than his previous books, partly in gratitude to Scribners and partly because, having made such a complete artistic statement, he seemed to be, temporarily, somewhat disinterested in money. The novel sold just over 20,000 copies, and, of its second printing of 3,000, there were still some languishing in Scribners' warehouse at the time of Fitzgerald's death. Even more ironically, it now sells more in a month than it did in Fitzgerald's lifetime, shifting over 300,000 copies annually in America alone.

## *Tender Is the Night*, New York, Scribners, 1934.

Published in 1934 and written over a nine-year period and in several different versions, *Tender Is the Night* was, arguably, Fitzgerald's own favourite among his works, and a book he called 'a confession of faith'. The corrupting influence of wealth and the clandestine sin of incest are at the dark heart of this powerful novel. Set on the French Riviera in the 1920s, it records the slow but inexorable decline of Dick Diver, a charismatic and handsome psychiatrist, and his marriage to a patient, the beautiful and wealthy Nicole Warren. The constant need to safeguard his wife's fragile sanity takes its toll on Dr Diver as he carries out his dual role of husband and counselor, virtually abandoning his true vocation. Whilst mindful of the fact that their elegant, cushioned lifestyle is due to his wife's income, he is also uncomfortably aware that her family have, in effect, purchased him to be her keeper.

As the novel progresses, she grows stronger and increasingly independent (a position bolstered by her money) whilst he, in turn, succumbs to alcoholism, the lures of a young actress and a growing malaise. Written at a time when his own wife Zelda had been committed to a Swiss sanatorium, suffering from schizophrenia, and his drinking was wildly out of control, Fitzgerald's last completed novel, despite its uneven structure, is exquisitely poignant. The final third of the book traces in graceful, almost imperceptible cadences, Dick's tragic descent from his wife's affections and the splendours of his former life. By the conclusion of this slow fade, he seems to have disappeared altogether, his existence dwindling to little more than hearsay. Not as polished as *The Great Gatsby* but, for all its imperfections, this is perhaps the better book.

## *The Last Tycoon*, New York, Scribners, 1941.

Possibly the saddest thing in a life besieged by tragedy was Fitzgerald's premature death, which occurred when he was a few weeks away from finishing his fifth novel. Set in Hollywood in the 1930s, this is the story of movie producer, Monroe Stahr, a character based largely on the legendary 'boy wonder', Irving Thalberg, who became head of production at Universal when he was just twenty, and who had died in 1936, aged thirty-seven. Fitzgerald had written 44,000 words of the book, and was probably about two thirds of the way through the first draft, intending to write another 20,000 words or so, when he died. Stahr meets a young English actress, Kathleen Moore, who is married, and, partly because she reminds him of his dead wife, Minna, he falls in love with her and they start having an affair. He is beset by problems, struggling to deal with financiers on one hand and labour leaders on the other, and is also aggravated by ill health, which threatens to cut short his illustrious career.

According to Fitzgerald's notes for the novel, Stahr's partner, Brady, plans to blackmail him, threatening to tell Kathleen's husband of their affair. Stahr has something on Brady, however, and after learning that his partner plans to have him killed, he decides to do the same, and arranges to have him murdered while he is away from Hollywood, flying east for business talks. On the plane, Stahr has second thoughts, and decides to cancel the killing by phoning from the next airport. The plane crashes, however, and Stahr dies before making the call and the murder takes place. Notes at the end of the unfinished novel indicate that a washed-up cowboy actor is mistakenly invited to be a pall-bearer at Stahr's funeral, and because of his mystified presence at this prestigious occasion, he is swamped with job offers. In Matthew J. Bruccoli's biography, *Some Sort of Epic Grandeur*, he reveals that, 'Fitzgerald's early idea for the conclusion was to have the plane wreck plundered by children whose characters would be shaped by the possessions they take', an absolutely stunning idea. Because of his death, we'll never know which ideas he would have chosen or how he would have expressed them. Edited and named by his friend, Edmund Wilson (Fitzgerald may have wanted to call it *The Love of the Last Tycoon: A Western; Stahr: A Romance* or *The Last of the Tycoons*), the novel, such as it is, is full of wonderful writing, but remains tantalizingly, tragically incomplete – just like the rest of Fitzgerald's life and work.

## *Trimalchio*, West III, James L W (Editor), Cambridge, Cambridge University Press, 2000.

Conceived throughout the summer of 1922 whilst Fitzgerald was putting his story collection, *Tales of the Jazz Age*, to bed, *The Great Gatsby* had a complex and protracted gestation. A year after his initial ideas, he had completed 18,000 words, most of which were discarded. Moving to France the following year, he re-thought the book and wrote it under the title *Trimalchio*, the name of the former slave and wealthy party host in the 2nd century Latin author Petronius's work, *Satyricon*. This edition, published for the first time in 2000, differs markedly from the finished version of *The Great Gatsby*, demonstrating just how extensive and skilful was Fitzgerald's editing and re-writing of the manuscript. Indecision seems to have been the order of the day for the author as he wrestled with the book, not committing himself to even the title until the eleventh hour. Fortunately for us, *Trimalchio in West Egg*; *Among the Ash Heaps and Millionaires*; *On the Road to West Egg* and *Gold-Hatted Gatsby* (getting there!) were all jettisoned in favour of the name that we know and love. In March, only a month away from publication, Fitzgerald actually wanted to change the title to either *Trimalchio* or *Gold-Hatted Gatsby*, and a few days later, even after Maxwell Perkins had told him that a 'change would cause bad delay and confusion', Fitzgerald cabled again to say that he was 'CRAZY ABOUT TITLE UNDER THE RED WHITE AND BLUE', but it was too late, and the famous title remained. This edition affords the lucky reader the thrill of experiencing the prototype of a masterpiece, a dress rehearsal for a work of art.

# The Stories

Fitzgerald's stories originally appeared in four volumes, each one published to capitalise on the success of a novel, so that *Flappers and Philosophers* followed *This Side of Paradise*, *Tales of the Jazz Age* followed *The Beautiful and Damned*, *All the Sad Young Men* followed *The Great Gatsby* and *Taps At Reveille* followed *Tender Is the Night*. Fitzgerald's stories are difficult to pin down, because they have appeared in so many different configurations and editions. Some of these volumes are readily available, while others are more obscure, but they're all worth tracking down.

*Flappers and Philosophers*, New York, Scribners, 1920.
*Tales of the Jazz Age*, New York, Scribners, 1922.
*All the Sad Young Men* New York, Scribners, 1926.
*Taps at Reveille*, New York, Scribners, 1935.

### *The Collected Short Stories*,
### London, Penguin, 2000.

With over forty stories ranging from the early New York masterpieces like *The Diamond as Big as the Ritz* to the mature, bleaker Hollywood pieces like *Crazy Sunday*, this probably represents the best of Fitzgerald's shorter work. The overall view one receives from this selection is that Fitzgerald wrote mainly of two things, love and money, with alcohol staggering not far behind. There is an impressive breadth of range here and the best of these stories (the majority of them, in fact) resonate with an emotional strength that remains unequalled. Alongside the charm, descriptive prowess, dry humour and dry martinis, lies an imposing sadness and a palpable sense of life's futility. This combination of art and heart is perhaps the key to Fitzgerald's impact and longevity as a writer. Among the many highlights are *Absolution* (a kind of forerunner to *The Great Gatsby*); *The Lees of Happiness*; *Bernice Bobs Her Hair*; *Babylon Revisited* and the sublime Armistice Day mini-epic *May Day*, which are all classics and proof that this is quite simply some of the finest writing of the twentieth century.

## *The Price Was High*, New York, Harcourt Brace Jovanovich, 1979.

Fitzgerald also balked at including stories in his collections that repeated material used in his novels, so that many of his stories weren't properly collected during his lifetime. Edited by Matthew J. Bruccoli, *The Price Was High* amasses fifty of these stories, including one, the appropriately-titled *On Your Own*, that had never been published before its appearance here. Some of these are wonderful, and some are entertaining, but standard Fitzgerald. All are worth reading. Bruccoli's fascinating comments on each story are a definite bonus.

### *Bits of Paradise*: Twenty-One New Stories, London, Bodley Head, 1973.

Edited by Bruccoli and Scottie Fitzgerald Smith, this is a kind of joint effort with stories by both Fitzgerald and Zelda, and ones that they both worked on.

### *The Rich Boy*, London, Hesperus Press, 2003.

Three of Fitzgerald's stories have been collected together in a bitter-sweet little volume and graced with an introduction by John Updike. The reason these three particular tales have been selected is because, as Updike shrewdly suggests, 'To Fitzgerald, money signals animal vitality, sexual success is part of its romance', and this trio eloquently conveys this. As well as the celebrated title story, this also includes *The Bridal Party* and *The Last of the Belles*.

### *The Basil and Josephine Stories*, New York, Scribners, 1973.

Edited by Jackson R Bryer and John Keuhl, this collection is Fitzgerald's wonderful recreation of his adolescence and early romance.

### *The Pat Hobby Stories*, New York, Scribners, 1962.

Edited by Arnold Gingrich, this consists of seventeen amusing tales about a gin-soaked Hollywood hack.

Although dashed off for pin money, they're definitely worth reading, if only to see how their cynical humour contrasts with the poignancy of *The Last Tycoon*. The stories are also Fitzgerald's last completed work.

# Non-Fiction and Letters

## *The Crack-Up*, New York, New Directions, 1945.

Edited by Fitzgerald's friend, Edmund Wilson, this consists of the three confessional pieces written for *Esquire* magazine in 1935 that polarised his friends, leaving them either full of admiration for his honesty or embarrassed by, and scornful of, his shamefulness. Maxwell Perkins was among the latter; hence Scribners did not publish this. Also included are some other essays, including his moving tribute to Ring Lardner, and a handful of stories.

## Bryer, Jackson R. & Barks, Cathy W. (Editors), *Dear Scott, Dearest Zelda*, New York, St Martins Press, 2002.

Beautifully assembled, this wonderful collection of the correspondence between Fitzgerald and his wife covers their whole life together (and apart). It includes telegrams announcing another instalment in Fitzgerald's early rise to fame, and letters ranging from all manner of vituperative accusations and talk of divorce to declarations of love that are almost childlike in their devotion and reverence.

**Bruccoli, Matthew J. (Editor),** *F. Scott Fitzgerald: A Life in Letters*, **New York, Scribners, 1994.**

One of the most fascinating impressions of Fitzgerald can be gleaned from his collected correspondence, and Bruccoli has done a fine job arranging it. Whether hastily scribbled or composed in Fitzgerald's customary exquisite prose, these missives provide an invaluable insight into the man and the writer behind the myth.

**Kuell, John & Bryer, Jackson R. (Editors),** *Dear Scott ~ Dear Max – the Fitzgerald–Perkins Correspondence*, **New York, Scribners, 1971.**

A fascinating collection of letters between an author and his editor, this reveals the evolution of Fitzgerald's literary career better than any other volume.

# Fitzgerald on Screen

Just as he struggled to bend his writing talent so that it would fit inside the rigid parameters of Hollywood scriptwriting in the 1920s and 1930s, Fitzgerald's work, although keenly sought after by producers, has always had a difficult time in its adaptation to the big screen. After *Head and Shoulders* was published in *The Saturday Evening Post*, Metro-Goldwyn-Mayer bought the film rights for $2,500, a breathtaking sum for the recently impoverished young writer. This was filmed in 1920–21 as *The Chorus Girl's Romance*, directed by William C. Dowlan and starring Viola Dana as Marcia Meadows. Dana also starred in *The Offshore Pirate*, directed by Dallas M. Fitzgerald (no relation). This was also bought for $2,500 by MGM, and taken from Fitzgerald's first story collection, *Flappers and Philosophers*. Between these two films, Twentieth Century Fox produced a film called *The Husband Hunter*, which was adapted from Fitzgerald's story *Myra Meets his Family*, directed by Howard M. Mitchell and starring Eileen Percy as Myra. This was published in *The Saturday Evening Post*, but excluded from *Flappers and Philosophers*, since Fitzgerald considered it to be too poor.

The next of his works to be filmed was Fitzgerald's second novel, *The Beautiful and Damned*, published in

March 1922 and for which the film rights were immediately bought by Warner Brothers. The film was directed by William A. Seiter and starred Kenneth Harlan as Anthony and Marie Prevost as Gloria. The film was apparently a dreary affair, which garnered poor reviews. James Gray in the St Paul Dispatch (which at one time might have been Fitzgerald's local paper) harshly described it as being 'one of the most horrific pictures of memory'.

Although one Hollywood producer talked of filming *This Side of Paradise* with Scott and Zelda Fitzgerald starring as Amory Blaine and Rosalind Connage (not such a crazy idea, since both were young, nice-looking and photogenic), nothing came of it. Famous Players bought the film rights in 1923 for $10,000, a price that also included hiring Fitzgerald to write the script, although his work was rejected (the first, but sadly not the last time that his writing for the screen was deemed unsuitable), and the film remained unproduced.

*The Great Gatsby* has been filmed four times: in 1926, 1949, 1974 and in an HBO version in 2001. The first, and silent, version was directed by Herbert Brenon and starred Warner Baxter as Gatsby, Lois Wilson as Daisy, Neil Hamilton as Nick Carraway, Hale Harrington as Tom Buchanan and William Powell, somewhat improbably cast, as George Wilson. Following the novel's successful stage adaptation and run on Broadway, Harold Ober had sold the rights to Paramount, with Fitzgerald pocketing $25,000 from the play and film sale. The film received mixed reviews, with one astute critic calling the novel 'one of the very best stories in modern American fiction', but dismissing the film as 'half way dull, half way cold and uninteresting'. In 1938, only two years before Fitzgerald's death, novelist John O'Hara, a friend and fellow carouser, tried to buy the rights to the book from Paramount, who owned them and refused to sell. Prompted by O'Hara's interest, the studio snapped into action, releasing the first sound version of the novel a mere eleven years later. It was directed by Elliott Nugent and starred Alan Ladd as Gatsby, Betty Field as Daisy, and Howard da Silva as George Wilson.

Fitzgerald's friend from Princeton, Edmund Wilson, the man whom he would call his 'artistic conscience', attended a preview showing of this version with Stanley Kauffman, a reviewer for *The New Republic*, and was asked by a publicity man from Paramount to what extent he had liked the film. 'Not very much, I'm afraid', was his candid reply. Twenty-five years later, in his review of the third version of the film, then being subjected to a frenzy of hype, Kauffman recalled the incident with Wilson. 'There are lots of reasons why I wish Wilson were still alive, but one of them is to hear his comments on the new Gatsby film. It makes the 1949 version and 1926 version before it (as far as I can remember it) look like twin pinnacles of art.'

The pre-publicity for this film was enormous, with an entire fashion movement, cunningly titled *The Great Gatsby Look*, launched a full year before the film was released – a curious move, since the look, presumably, would have been somewhat out of fashion by the time the film finally graced the silver screen. Included in this bonanza were Gatsby and Daisy boutiques in various major American department stores, a shop called 'Great

Scott' in Bloomingdale's New York City branch, and features in *Time* magazine and *Vogue*, where Fitzgerald's essay, *Echoes of the Jazz Age*, was reprinted, alongside location stills from the forthcoming movie. In the magazine, Paramount Promotions Director, Charles Glenn, modestly suggested that the studio's humble aim was merely 'to *Gatsbyize* the entire country'. Equally modest was Paramount's original offer for the film rights, owned by Fitzgerald's daughter, Frances Scott Fitzgerald Smith, but the hoped for sum of $130,000 was bumped up to an impressive $350,000, which was paid outright, as well as a share of the profits. At least she had more financial sense than her father.

The cost of making the film is thought to be somewhere in the region of six to seven million dollars, a fairly expensive region. Such large sums are ironic, given that the principal themes are, of course, money and love. The film was directed by Jack Clayton, scripted by Francis Ford Coppola and starred Robert Redford as Gatsby, Mia Farrow as Daisy, Sam Waterston as Nick Carraway, Bruce Dern as Tom, Karen Black as Myrtle Wilson, Scott Wilson as George Wilson and Howard da Silva, who had played George Wilson in the 1949 version, as gambler Meyer Wolfsheim, 'the man who fixed the World Series'. Retaining the baseball terminology, the film struck out with most critics and was generally considered to be a massive disappointment and much too long, with the crystal-clear brevity and perfectly-honed structure of the novel abandoned in favour of a lengthy and slow parade of colourful, but bland, imagery, endless tracking shots, repetitive perspectives and a voice-over confirming what the audience had already been shown (and shown again!) on the screen.

Rumour has it that Marlon Brando and Warren Beatty turned down the part of Gatsby, and that Jack Nicholson either turned it down or was rejected for the part. Nicholson's buddy, screenwriter Robert Towne was apparently offered $125,000 to write the screenplay for the film, but felt he couldn't top Fitzgerald's novel, and so accepted $25,000 to write his own story instead. This became *Chinatown*, a brilliant film, which Nicholson did star in. Another rumour states that the original script had been written by Truman Capote, in whose version Nick Carraway was an effete homosexual and Jordan Baker an aggressive lesbian. Fired by the studio for his script, Capote sued them, but settled out of court for $110,000. The screenwriting duties were then assumed by Coppola, who scripted the film in three weeks, although his screenplay was heavily doctored by director Clayton.

The HBO version was made in 2001, and was directed by Robert Markowitz, with the teleplay written by John McLaughlin. The cast included Toby Stephens as Gatsby, Paul Rudd as Nick Carraway, Mira Sorvino as Daisy and Martin Donovan as Tom Buchanan.

*Tender Is the Night* was filmed in 1962. Directed by Henry King, with a script by Henry Moffatt, it starred Jennifer Jones as Nicole Diver and Jason Robards, Jr as Dick, with Tom Ewell as Abe North, Jill St John as Rosemary Hoyt and Joan Fontaine as Nicole's sister, Baby Warren. Film producer Michael Korda appears, uncredited, as an 'Italian Gentleman'. It ran for almost two and a half hours, way too long for the time, and received poor reviews. The novel was also adapted as a six-part television series in 1985, scripted by Dennis Potter and directed by Robert Knights. The series was received very well, garnering perhaps the best reviews of a Fitzgerald screen adaptation, and its cast featured Peter Strauss and Mary Steenburgen as Dick and Nicole Diver, John Heard as Abe North, Sean Young as Rosemary Hoyt and Kate Harper as Baby Warren. Henry King also directed a film based on a book called *Beloved Infidel*, published in 1958 and co-written by Sheilah Graham and Gerold Frank. The book was an autobiography that covered her turbulent, early years in England and her equally turbulent relationship with Fitzgerald. It was made into a film in 1959, and starred Gregory Peck as Fitzgerald and Deborah Kerr as Graham. King also directed three films based on works by Fitzgerald's old friend and literary rival, Ernest Hemingway: *The Snows of Kilimanjaro* (1952), *The Sun Also Rises* (1957) and (uncredited) *The Old Man and the Sea* (1958).

Fitzgerald's last novel, *The Last Tycoon*, the unfinished book about Hollywood, was filmed in 1976 and directed by Elia Kazan, with a screenplay by Harold Pinter. The all-star cast was headed by Robert De Niro as Monroe Stahr, the studio head of production, whom Fitzgerald had based on Irving Thalberg, Ingrid Boulting as Kathleen Moore and Theresa Russell as Cecilia Brady, the daughter of Stahr's business partner. The supporting cast included John Carradine as Pat Brady, the crooked partner; Ray Milland as Fleishacker, the studio's lawyer in New York; Donald Pleasance as an English novelist trying make a career at scriptwriting and Dana Andrews as Wylie White, a

Hollywood hack writer. Perhaps to atone for his absence in *The Great Gatsby*, Jack Nicholson had a brief, but highly effective cameo as Brimmer, a representative from the Communist Party, who is in the process of organising the writers' union when he tussles with Stahr. The film received mixed, mostly poor, reviews. Judith Crist in the *Saturday Review* was of the opinion that the film was 'killed with reverence', whilst, in *The New Yorker*, Pauline Kael wrote: 'The characters are so enervated that *The Last Tycoon* is a vampire movie after the vampires have left.'

*The Last of the Belles* was a TV film shown in 1974 and directed by George Schaefer, and was a curious mixture. Part of it was based on Fitzgerald's story of the same name, written in 1929, and a semi-fictional account of his meeting with Zelda in Montgomery, Alabama in 1918. The other part was a kind of biopic of the Fitzgeralds and their troubled life in the 1930s, having returned to America from Europe. Richard Chamberlain played Fitzgerald, Blythe Danner played Zelda and Susan Sarandon played Ailie Calhoun, the heroine in Fitzgerald's story. The screenplay was written by James Costigan, who also scripted another TV movie in 1976 called *F Scott Fitzgerald in Hollywood*, a dramatised account of two of the author's attempts to crack the film industry. The first was in 1927, when he was at the peak of his fame, and the last was ten years later, when he was heavily in debt, alcoholic and struggling with what he called his 'emotional bankruptcy', a condition that he felt was rendering him incapable of writing. The film was directed by Anthony Page and starred Jason Miller as Fitzgerald, Tuesday Weld as Zelda, Julia Foster as gossip columnist Sheilah Graham,

Dolores Sutton as Dorothy Parker and a young James Woods as a character named Leonard 'Lenny' Schoenfeld.

Fitzgerald's own attempts at scriptwriting were almost all fairly unsuccessful. His first was in 1927 when he was hired to write the screenplay for a Constant Talmadge film, *Lipstick*, a comedy about a flapper. He was paid $3,500 to write it, with the promise of another $12,500 when his script was accepted. It wasn't, and, as they had spent more than the $3,500 advance, he and Zelda left Hollywood low in spirits and funds, fighting with each other as they went east. Fitzgerald had also fought with Talmadge while writing the script, which couldn't have helped. His next job in Hollywood was in 1931, when he was hired by MGM to write a script of Katherine Brush's novel, *Red-Headed Woman*. The job paid $750 a week for six weeks' work, but when Fitzgerald demurred, he was offered $1,200 a week. He finished the work a week early and went home for Christmas. His script was rejected and Anita Loos wrote a new screenplay.

His third and final attempt saw him working on a number of films, but the only screen credit he achieved was for *Three Comrades*, an MGM film based on a novel by Erich Maria Remarque, author of the World War I classic *All Quiet on the Western Front*. Directed by Frank Borzage and starring Robert Taylor, Margaret Sullavan, Franchot Tone and Robert Young, this is the only script by Fitzgerald that seems to have survived largely intact. He wanted sole screen credit for it, although he didn't get this, mainly due to producer Joseph Mankiewicz changing his script, and the final credit read that the film was written by Fitzgerald and E. E. Paramore, Jr. Ironically, this was Ted

Paramore, an old acquaintance from Princeton whom the writer had satirically depicted in *The Beautiful and Damned*, and with whom he quarrelled badly over the screenplay. In a letter to his erstwhile collaborator, he claimed that Paramore was rewriting it in language befitting a Western, and not a tragic love story set in interwar Europe, with Fascism on the rise. He also foolishly sent an angry letter to Mankiewicz, a headstrong man who had a reputation for annoying writers by often brutally revising their screenplays. A review of the film in the *New York Daily Mirror* commented on the screenplay, reporting that 'there was grapevine news that it was one of the best scripts ever turned in at Metro'. The screenplay credit, even though it was shared with a man whom he considered something of a rival, if an inferior one, was the first and last that Fitzgerald ever received.

While he was working on his final novel, *The Last Tycoon*, he was commissioned to write a script based on his story *Babylon Revisited* by an independent producer, Leslie Cowan. Regarded as one of Fitzgerald's classic stories and one of the finest written during an increasingly turbulent period in his life, it also had a complex and, inevitably, rather ironic, cinematic history, and its eventual evolution from page to screen, spanning around twenty-three years, seems to sum up its author's own tangled and fraught relationship with Hollywood. Fitzgerald's screenplay, now called *Cosmopolitan*, was never filmed, and Cowan, having paid $6,000 for the rights and Fitzgerald's scripting work, sold it, years after the author's death, for a cool $40,000 to MGM, who used it to make *The Last Time I Saw Paris*, in 1954. This film was scripted by Philip G. Epstein, Julius J.

Epstein and Richard Brooks, was directed by Brooks and starred Elizabeth Taylor, Van Johnson, Walter Pidgeon and Donna Reed. Needless to say, it's totally unrecognisable from Fitzgerald's original story.

# Biographies

There have been scores of biographies of Fitzgerald, but these are some of the best.

Bruccoli, Matthew J., *Some Sort of Epic Grandeur*, New York, Harcourt Brace Jovanovich, 1981.
By far the best biography of its subject, this is a brilliant, incisive and authoritative study by the foremost Fitzgerald scholar. Perceptive, meticulously researched and movingly written, this casts an imperious shadow over the rest of the crowded field.

Mizener, Arthur, *The Far Side of Paradise*, Boston, Houghton Mifflin, 1951.
Published in 1951, this readable biography was the first study of Fitzgerald, but rather suffers for being so, in comparison with later works.

Mellow, James R., *Invented Lives – F Scott and Zelda Fitzgerald*, Houghton Mifflin, Boston, 1987.
This is a fine biography of the pair, which starts from the intriguing premise that they invented their own lives.

Le Vot, André, *F Scott Fitzgerald – A Biography*, New York, Doubleday, 1983.
A compassionate and sympathetic look at Fitzgerald from a professor of American literature at the Sorbonne.

Turnbull, Andrew, *Scott Fitzgerald*, New York, Scribners, 1962.
Highly readable account of Fitzgerald's life and work from someone who, as a boy, was befriended by Fitzgerald in the 1930s.

Donaldson, Scott, *Hemingway vs. Fitzgerald*, New York, Overlook Press, 1999.
Subtitled *The Rise and Fall of a Literary Friendship*, this is a fascinating account of the relationship between these rival authors and alcoholics, and Donaldson has produced a convincing and moving record of two of the 20th century's most enduring and tragic literary giants.

Graham, Sheilah, *The Real F Scott Fitzgerald*, New York, Grosset & Dunlap, 1976.

Graham, Sheilah & Frank, Gerold, *Beloved Infidel*, New York, Holt, Rinehart & Winston, 1958.

Ring, Frances Kroll, *Against the Current*, San Francisco, Creative Arts Book Company, 1985.

Latham, Aaron, *Crazy Sundays – F Scott Fitzgerald in Hollywood*, New York, Viking, 1971.

These all cover Fitzgerald's final period, when he was trying to be a successful scriptwriter. Graham's books have plenty of accounts of Fitzgerald's best and worst behaviour; Frances Kroll Ring was his secretary and provides a warm, charming memoir of her experiences, while Latham's is probably the most objective.

# Critical Works

There are countless critical works on Fitzgerald. Here are just a few which are particularly rewarding for the Fitzgerald fan.

Mizener, Arthur (Editor), *F. Scott Fitzgerald – A Collection of Critical Essays*, New Jersey, Prentice-Hall, 1963.

Kazin, Alfred (Editor), *F. Scott Fitzgerald – The Man and His Work*, Cleveland, World, 1951.

Bruccoli, Matthew J., *The Last of the Novelists: F. Scott Fitzgerald and The Last Tycoon*, Carbondale & Edwardsville, Southern Illinois University Press, 1977.

Bryer, Jackson R, *F. Scott Fitzgerald – The Critical Reception*, New York, Burt Franklin, 1978.

Cowley, Malcolm & Robert (Editors), *Fitzgerald & the Jazz Age*, New York, Scribners, 1966.

Gallo, Rose Adrienne, *F. Scott Fitzgerald*, New York, Frederick Ungar Publishing, 1978.

# Novels Written About Fitzgerald

Handler, David, *The Man Who Would Be F. Scott Fitzgerald*, New York, Doubleday, 1990.
This is an entertaining crime novel about a talented young writer in 1980s New York, who, like Fitzgerald, has a huge success with his first novel and achieves overnight fame. Fitzgerald and, in particular, *The Great Gatsby*, are mentioned throughout.

Jackson, Charles, *The Lost Weekend*, New York, Farrar & Rinehart, 1944.
Set in the twilight world of 1940s New York with its ubiquitous smoky saloons, this bleak, unremitting and arresting novel is the story of Don Birnam, a talented, self-obsessed alcoholic and his irrevocable journey towards what could be his final bender. Made into a successful film in 1945, this is, unfortunately, Jackson's only published work and, among its many highlights, is an affectionately ironic cameo appearance by Fitzgerald near the book's conclusion.

Aldridge, James, *One Last Glimpse*, New York, Little Brown, 1977.
This is a fictional account of a trip taken by Fitzgerald and

Hemingway in the 1920s in France. As well as the two literary giants, Zelda, Gerald and Sara Murphy and Hemingway's wife, Hadley, also appear.

Schulberg, Budd, *The Disenchanted*, New York, Random House, 1950.
Selected by Anthony Burgess in his book, *99 Novels: The Best in English Since 1939*, this is a fictional account of the disastrous journey made by Fitzgerald and Schulberg when they were co-writing the script for the film, *Winter Carnival*. Schulberg claimed, rather unconvincingly, that his character, Manley Halliday, was based on several writers in Hollywood, amongst whom one happened to be Fitzgerald.

# Fitzgerald on the Web

Putting Fitzgerald's name into a search engine brings up a mass of websites as big as the Ritz, but these are a few of the more interesting ones.

http://www.sc.edu/fitzgerald/
http://www.fitzgeraldsociety.org/
http://www.online-literature.com/fitzgerald/
http://people.brandeis.edu/~teuber/fitzgeraldbio.html
http://faculty.millikin.edu/~moconner.hum.faculty.mu/e232/fitzgeraldbio.html
http://www.findadeath.com/Deceased/F/F.Scott%20Fitzgerald/f.htm

# Books By and About Zelda Fitzgerald

Much of Zelda's story can be read, albeit in fictional form, in her only novel, *Save Me the Waltz*, but there are several biographies that tell her side of the story. *The Collected Writings of Zelda Fitzgerald*, edited by Matthew J. Bruccoli and Mary Gordon, is the best volume of her work, since it includes the novel, her play, *Scandalabra*, and several stories and non-fiction pieces.

Fitzgerald, Zelda, *The Collected Writings of Zelda Fitzgerald*, Alabama, University of Alabama Press, 1997.

Mayfield, Sara, *Exiles from Paradise – Zelda and Scott Fitzgerald*, New York, Delacorta Press, 1971.

Milford, Nancy, *Zelda Fitzgerald*, New York, Harper & Row, 1970.

Cline, Sally, *Zelda Fitzgerald – Her Voice in Paradise*, New York, Arcade Publishing, 2003.

Taylor, Kendall, *Sometimes Madness is Wisdom – Zelda and Scott Fitzgerald: A Marriage*, New York, Ballantine Books, 2001.

Meade, Marion, *Bobbed Hair & Bathtub Gin – Writers Running Wild in the Twenties – Zelda Fitzgerald, Edna St Vincent Millay, Dorothy Parker and Edna Ferber*, New York, Nan A Talese/Doubleday, 2004.

# Books on Other People in Fitzgerald's Life

These are books on or by many of the people who were the supporting cast in the drama that was the Fitzgeralds' life.

## The Murphys

Tomkins, Calvin, *Living Well is the Best Revenge*, New York, Viking, 1971.

Vaill, Amanda, *Everybody Was So Young – Gerald and Sara Murphy: A Lost Generation Love Story*, Boston, Houghton Mifflin, 1998.

## Ernest Hemingway

Baker, Carlos, *Hemingway*, New Jersey, Princeton University Press, 1972.

Meyers, Jeffrey, *Hemingway – a Biography*, California, Borgo Press, 1991.

Hemingway, Ernest, *A Moveable Feast*, New York, Scribners, 1964.

# Maxwell Perkins

Berg, A. Scott, *Maxwell Perkins – Editor of Genius*, New York, Congdon/Dutton, 1978.

Cowley, Malcolm, *Unshaken Friend: A Profile of Maxwell Perkins*, Colorado, Roberts Rinehart, 1985.

Bruccoli, Matthew J. & Baughman, Judith S. (Editors), *The Sons of Maxwell Perkins – Letters of F. Scott Fitzgerald, Ernest Hemingway, Thomas Wolfe and Their Editor*, South Carolina, University of South Carolina Press, 2004.

| | | |
|---|---|---|
| 1903047773 | Agatha Christie  Mark Campbell  4.99 | |
| 1903047706 | Alan Moore  Lance Parkin  3.99 | |
| 1903047528 | Alchemy & Alchemists  Sean Martin  3.99 | |
| 1903047005 | Alfred Hitchcock  Paul Duncan  4.99 | |
| 1903047722 | American Civil War  Phil Davies  3.99 | |
| 1903047730 | American Indian Wars  Howard Hughes  3.99 | |
| 1903047757 | Ancient Greece  Mike Paine  3.99 | |
| 1903047714 | Ang Lee  Ellen Cheshire  3.99 | |
| 1903047463 | Animation  Mark Whitehead  4.99 | |
| 1903047676 | Audrey Hepburn  Ellen Cheshire  3.99 | |
| 190304779X | The Beastie Boys  Richard Luck  3.99 | |
| 1904048196 | The Beatles  Paul Charles  3.99 | |
| 1903047854 | The Beat Generation  Jamie Russell  3.99 | |
| 1903047366 | Billy Wilder  Glenn Hopp  3.99 | |
| 1903047919 | Bisexuality  Angie Bowie  3.99 | |
| 1903047749 | Black Death  Sean Martin  3.99 | |
| 1903047587 | Blaxploitation Films  Mikel J Koven  3.99 | |
| 1903047455 | Bollywood  Ashok Banker  3.99 | |
| 1903047129 | Brian de Palma  John Ashbrook  3.99 | |
| 1903047579 | Bruce Lee  Simon B Kenny  3.99 | |
| 1904048978 | Bruce Springsteen  4.99 | |
| 190404803X | Carry On Films  Mark Campbell  4.99 | |
| 1904048048 | Classic Radio Comedy  Nat Coward  3.99 | |
| 1903047811 | Clint Eastwood  Michael Carlson  3.99 | |
| 190304703X | Coen Brothers  Cheshire/Ashbrook  4.99 | |
| 1903047307 | Conspiracy Theories  Robin Ramsay  3.99 | |
| 1904048099 | Creative Writing  Neil Nixon  3.99 | |
| 1903047536 | The Crusades  Mike Paine  3.99  (R/P) | |
| 1903047285 | Cyberpunk  Andrew M Butler  3.99 | |
| 1903047269 | David Cronenberg  John Costello  3.99 | |
| 1903047064 | David Lynch  Le Blanc/Odell  3.99 | |
| 1903047196 | Doctor Who  Mark Campbell  4.99 | |
| 1904048277 | Do Your Own PR  Richard Milton  3.99 | |
| 190304751X | Feminism  Susan Osborne  3.99 | |
| 1903047633 | Film Music  Paul Tonks  3.99 | |
| 1903047080 | Film Noir  Paul Duncan  3.99 | |
| 1904048080 | Film Studies  Andrew M Butler  4.99 | |
| 190304748X | Filming on a Microbudget NE  Paul Hardy  4.99 | |
| 190304765X | French New Wave  Chris Wiegand  4.99 | |
| 1903047544 | Freud & Psychoanalysis  Nick Rennison  3.99 | |
| 1904048218 | Georges Simenon  David Carter  3.99 | |
| 1903047943 | George Lucas  James Clarke  3.99 | |
| 1904048013 | German Expressionist Films  Paul Cooke  3.99 | |
| 1904048161 | Globalisation  Steven P McGiffen  3.99 | |
| 1904048145 | Hal Hartley  Jason Wood  3.99 | |
| 1904048110 | Hammer Films  John McCarty  3.99 | |
| 1903047994 | History of Witchcraft  Lois Martin  3.99 | |
| 1903047404 | Hitchhiker's Guide  M J Simpson  4.99 | |
| 1903047072 | Hong Kong's Heroic Bloodshed  Martin Fitzgerald  3.99  (R/P) | |
| 1903047382 | Horror Films  Le Blanc/Odell  3.99 | |
| 1903047692 | Jack the Ripper  Whitehead/Rivett  3.99 | |
| 1903047102 | Jackie Chan  Le Blanc/Odell  3.99 | |
| 1903047951 | James Cameron  Brian J Robb  3.99 | |
| 1903047242 | Jane Campion  Ellen Cheshire  3.99 | |
| 1904048188 | Jethro Tull  Raymond Benson  3.99 | |
| 1903047374 | John Carpenter  Le Blanc/Odell  3.99 | |

| | | |
|---|---|---|
| 1904048285 | The Knights Templar Sean Martin 9.99 hb | |
| 1903047250 | Krzystzof Kieslowski Monika Maurer 3.99 (R/P) | |
| 1903047609 | Laurel & Hardy Brian J Robb 3.99 | |
| 1903047803 | The Madchester Scene Richard Luck 3.99 | |
| 1903047315 | Marilyn Monroe Paul Donnelley 3.99 | |
| 1903047668 | Martin Scorsese Paul Duncan 4.99 | |
| 1903047595 | The Marx Brothers Mark Bego 3.99 | |
| 1903047846 | Michael Mann Mark Steensland 3.99 | |
| 1903047641 | Mike Hodges Mark Adams 3.99 | |
| 1903047498 | Nietzsche Travis Elborough 3.99 (R/P) | |
| 1903047110 | Noir Fiction Paul Duncan 3.99 | |
| 1904048226 | Nuclear Paranoia C Newkey-Burden 3.99 | |
| 1903047927 | Oliver Stone Michael Carlson 3.99 | |
| 1903047048 | Orson Welles Martin Fitzgerald 3.99 | |
| 1904048366 | Quentin Tarantino 4.99 | |
| 1903047293 | Philip K Dick Andrew M Butler 3.99 | |
| 1904048242 | Postmodernism Andrew M Butler 3.99 | |
| 1903047560 | Ridley Scott Brian Robb 3.99 | |
| 1903047838 | The Rise of New Labour Robin Ramsay 3.99 | |
| 1904048102 | Roger Corman Mark Whitehead 3.99 | |
| 1903047897 | Roman Polanski Daniel Bird 3.99 | |
| 1903047447 | Science Fiction Films 4.99 | |
| 1903047412 | Sergio Leone Michael Carlson 3.99 | |
| 1903047684 | Sherlock Holmes Mark Campbell 3.99 | |
| 1903047277 | Slasher Movies Mark Whitehead 3.99 | |
| 1904048072 | Spike Lee Darren Arnold 3.99 | |
| 1903047013 | Stanley Kubrick Paul Duncan 3.99 | |
| 190304782X | Steven Soderbergh Jason Wood 3.99 | |
| 1903047439 | Steven Spielberg James Clarke 4.99 | |
| 1903047331 | Stock Market Essentials Victor Cuadra 3.99 | |
| 1904048064 | Succeed in Music Business Paul Charles 3.99 | |
| 1903047765 | Successful Sports Agent Mel Stein 3.99 | |
| 1903047145 | Terry Gilliam John Ashbrook 3.99 | |
| 1903047390 | Terry Pratchett Andrew M Butler 3.99 | |
| 1903047625 | Tim Burton Le Blanc/Odell 4.99 | |
| 190404817X | Tintin J M & R Lofficier 3.99 | |
| 1903047889 | UFOs Neil Nixon 3.99 | |
| 1904048250 | The Universe Richard Osborne 9.99 hb | |
| 1904048358 | Urban Legends 4.99 | |
| 190304717X | Vampire Films Le Blanc/Odell 3.99 | |
| 190404820X | Videogaming Flatley & French 3.99 | |
| 1903047935 | Vietnam War Movies Jamie Russell 3.99 | |
| 1904048129 | Who Shot JFK? Robin Ramsay 3.99 | |
| 1904048056 | William Shakespeare Ian Nichols 3.99 | |
| 1903047056 | Woody Allen Martin Fitzgerald 3.99 | |
| 1903047471 | Writing a Screenplay John Costello 4.99 | |

Or browse all our titles at www.pocketessentials.com

Available from all good bookshops or send a cheque to: Pocket Essentials (Dept SS), P.O. Box 394, Harpenden, Herts, AL5 1XJ. Please make cheques payable to 'Oldcastle Books', add 50p for postage and packing for each book in the UK and £1 elsewhere.

US customers can send $8.95 plus $1.95 postage and packing for each book payable to; Trafalgar Square Publishing, PO Box 257, Howe Hill, North Pomfret, Vermont 05053, USA email tsquare@sover.net

Customers worldwide can order online at www.pocketessentials.com